HOW 2 FOCUS:
The Pitchers Zone

Innovative Ideas used by MLB Pitching
Stars

By

Dr. Bill Harrison

with Ryan Harrison

ISBN-10: 1533087199

ISBN-13: 978-1533087195

William D. Harrison, Laguna Beach, California

SlowTheGameDown, LLC.

1100 South Coast Highway, Suite 201

Laguna Beach, CA. 92651

(866) 627.5400

www.SlowTheGameDown.com

HOW 2 FOCUS:
The Pitchers Zone

Innovative Ideas used by MLB Pitching Stars

By

Dr. Bill Harrison

with Ryan Harrison

"What I learned from Dr. Harrison had a significant impact on my career. I recommend this book to every pitcher so he too can learn how to maximize his capability."

GREG MADDUX, Baseball Hall of Fame

How2Focus: **The Pitchers Zone**

What Others Have Said:

"I suspect I was the first Major League pitcher in history, beginning in 1972, to be trained on the mental side of pitching. What I learned from Dr. Harrison vaulted me from out of a pack of 75 pitchers who also wanted to pitch in the major leagues. Prior to this training, I used to sweat and work just 'way too hard.' Learning to use my brain allowed me to work easier and smarter, because I learned how to totally focus on my only task at hand. It was rather amazing how focused I became on the mound, as years later I was diagnosed as having ADHD. Dr. Harrison's approach helped me overcome the effects of ADHD when I pitched."

MARK LITTELL, 9 -year MLB Pitcher

"Every pitcher and every pitching coach need to learn what is presented here by the Harrison's. This emphasis will enhance everything they do. I used this information with my pitchers at Fresno State and we had some very good pitchers. If this book had been available I would have had every one of my pitchers study it, I would ask them questions about it and I am sure they would have been even better."

BOB BENNETT, Hall of Fame Collegiate Baseball Coach

"These ideas helped me have a long career as it helped the careers of most of my Chicago Cubs pitching staff members. I was a teammate of Greg Maddux, saw him apply these ideas and saw him go from being very good to becoming a Cy Young winner."

CHUCK McELROY, 13-year MLB Pitcher

"How2Focus: The Pitcher's Zone has something for every pitcher. Utilized properly a pitcher can use these ideas and improve their pitch command. I know, because they worked for me."

BOB SCANLON, 9-year MLB Pitcher

"We have been very fortunate to have the Harrison's a part of our program for the last 6 seasons. Their knowledge, techniques, and practices with vision have been an integral part of UCLA Baseball. Our players have benefitted greatly each year and have learned how to implement their information into their daily baseball routines."

JOHN SAVAGE

UCLA Baseball Head Coach

2013 National Champions

2011 & 2012 & 2015 Pac-12 Champions

"How2Focus: The Pitcher's Zone helped me a lot. As promised my pitch command improved markedly after using these ideas. I reduced my mistakes and began to win even when I didn't have my best stuff."

High School Senior Pitcher

Contents

Contents (Continued):

Author's Note

Because this is a nonacademic narration, we don't feel it is necessary to footnote or provide a comprehensive bibliography of resources. But we do want to include the name of authors who were influential in our developing this knowledge-base and our basic philosophy:

Larry Colton, *Southern League*

Tim Wendell, *High Heat*

Steve Cameron, *George Brett – The Last of a Breed*

Art Stewart, *Scouting*

Mel Didier, *Podnuh – Let Me Tell You a Story*

Daniel Coyle, *The Talent Code*

Harry Dunlop, *50 Years in a Kids Game*

Jack McKeon, *Jack of All Trades* and *I'm Just Getting Started*

Syd Thrift, *The Game According to Syd*

Shawn Green, *The Way of Baseball*

Larry Miller, *Exploring the Zone*

Vivien Saunders, *Advanced Golf*

Charlie Lau with Alfred Glossbrenner, *The Art of Hitting .300*

Bob Bennett, *A Passion for the Game* and *Playing Like Champions*

Michael Lewis, *Moneyball*

Rickie Henderson and John Shea, Offbase--*Confessions of a Thief*

Orel Hershiser with Jerry B. Jenkins, *Out of the Blue*

John Schuerholz with Larry Guest, *Built to Win*

Don Weiskopf, *Complete Baseball Handbook: Strategies and Techniques for Winning*

How2Focus: **The Pitchers Zone**

Foreword

By

Larry Colton

Former MLB Pitcher and current Book Author

Larry Colton was a teammate with Dr. Bill Harrison at the University of California at Berkeley in 1963 and 1964. After graduating from the University of California at Berkeley in 1964, Larry pitched in professional baseball for six years, including a brief stint with the Philadelphia Phillies. Following his baseball career, he has taught high school, worked for Nike, and been a writer. Between 1976 and 2000, his magazine articles appeared in publications such as Esquire, New York Times Magazine, Sports Illustrated, and Ladies Home Journal. He is the author of five books: Idol Time; Goat Brothers (a main selection for the Book of the Month Club); Counting Coup (winner of the Frankfurt e-book of the year award and a Pulitzer nominee); No Ordinary Joes; and Southern League. Additionally, he is the founder and former executive director of two non-profit programs: Community of Writers, a non-profit program to improve writing instruction and student achievement in Oregon schools; and Wordstock, the acclaimed Portland Book Festival.

I was a pro baseball player, even making it briefly to the big leagues, and when I say briefly, I'm talking about a Tuesday. I managed to make it that far mostly on natural ability rather than on commitment, discipline and focus. I played with and against guys with less natural talent and less common sense than the Three Stooges, and yet they'd be 100 percent zeroed in, no thoughts of their next fishing trip cluttering their focus. They had long, productive big league careers. Not me. I'd stand on the mound scoping out the girl behind the third base dugout or wondering why we'd just bombed Cambodia. My career was over in a flash. It shouldn't have been; because I had a "howitzer" for an arm.

Why am I writing the preface to this book? Well, for one thing, Bill and I go back a long way together - he was my college roommate and we were ace hurlers on the Cal baseball team. He was really good, and he was focused. I was not. If he had not ended his pitching career with a severe shoulder injury, I am sure he was good enough to have also pitched in the show.

If I had had this book, and taken the time to study it, I likely would have had a long prosperous MLB career. I lasted 89 days with the Philadelphia Phillies in 1967 and went 2-2 in 40 innings.

I wish today I could say "I pitched 90 days" because one more day and I would have received what would have been for me a significant signing bonus. All in all, I pitched 7 years in the minor leagues, 4 of which were at the AAA level and 89 days in the MLB.

There're many moments in my baseball career that I wish I'd had Dr. Harrison's training. But there's one that stands out. It was August 1968. I was pitching in an AAA game in San Diego, and while I was standing on the mound, I heard the crowd cheer for no apparent reason. When I turned and glanced at the giant message board in right field, I saw the announcement that Hubert Humphrey had just won the Democratic nomination at the Chicago Convention, the one with all the riots and beatings. (I had been a Bobby Kennedy fan, and then after he got gunned down, I switched allegiance to Eugene McCarthy...anybody but Humphrey and more of the failed policies of LBJ in Vietnam.) I just stood there on the mound, staring at the message board, pissed off, oblivious to the fact that the bases were loaded. When I finally stepped back on the rubber, the hitter, whom I'd struck out his previous three times at bat, launched my next pitch, a brain-dead fastball right down Central Avenue, into the upper deck in left field, a grand salami, living proof that focus is everything.

It's too late for Dr. Harrison to help my baseball career, but I have every reason to believe that he's going to help yours.

I also think he's going to turn my pitiful golf game around. I just wish I hadn't waited so long. I can't count the times I've said that the trouble with my golf game is between my ears. Walking down the fairway, my mind wanders into other zip codes and irritating things I can't control – the Seahawks blowing the Super Bowl, Ted Cruz's latest lunacy - anything but my next shot. It's the same thing I did when I pitched all those years

And when I do get ready to hit the ball, I'm filled with negative swing thoughts – don't slice it into the water, don't chunk it into that trap, and whatever you do, stupid, don't hook it out of bounds. It's paralysis by analysis – a thousand swing thoughts cluttering my mind - get properly aligned, keep my head down, take it back slow, turn my shoulder, follow through. By the time I swing, whatever athleticism I have left is gone like pie on my plate.

I am going to start working with Dr. Bill Harrison on my golf game. I know this is all going to change because how do I know that? I fully expect him to work a similar miracle with my golf game. I mean, he helped George Brett and Greg Maddux, didn't he?

In truth, I was a nitwit my entire athletic life. Maybe it's time for me to get better.

But realistically, 89 days in the show was great. But if I would have had the insights and approach that Dr. Harrison shares in this book I know I would have had some MLB years instead of just 89 days. Frankly, as a result, I have lived with a lot of frustration,

I suggest you study and apply so you won't share the same frustration.

Preface

By Jack McKeon

I first met Dr. Bill Harrison in January 1972. I was preparing to manage the Kansas City Royals AAA team, the Omaha Royals, in the upcoming American Association season.

At that time in my career, I thought I had seen or heard everything related to baseball. But I was wrong. Once you read this book, I think you will agree that you hadn't already learned, seen or heard everything either.

This book has many great true stories, humor, insights previously not known about players, meaningful demonstrations, and specific steps to follow to improve your pitching performance. What more could one ask for?

At the time I met Bill, I had been in baseball since 1949, thirty-three years either as a player or a manager. I had managed for 16 years, the prior 6 in AAA. After I graduated from high school, I then played 5 years for the Pirates and then bounced around for 5 more seasons with the Red Sox, Orioles, and Senators.

I was a pretty good minor league catcher, but I was a .210 hitter. I ran a game so well that in 1955, at age 24, I became a player-manager for a Baltimore Orioles Low B League Team. I wasn't highly gifted physically. Most certainly I wasn't a five-tool player. But I was pretty tough mentally. I suspect growing up in the depression years in New Jersey helped me be tough.

Though he was an eye doctor, I found him to be a focus coach. In fact, I think he was a baseball thinking coach. Our players ended up focusing better and thinking better. In fact, it seemed to me that everything he taught about vision directly affected the mental side of the game.

In 1972, Bill introduced to our pitchers many new insights that helped them perform better when they were under pressure. Up to that time I had seen a lot of pitchers look great in the bullpen, but at game time, their talent rarely showed up. That changed with the players Bill worked with.

Working with Bill gave me an understanding of how the pitcher's body and their brain worked together. He emphasized they needed to control their eyes because their eyes guided their brain which guided their body. I learned it to be true.

During the years, I managed the Royals, Athletics, Padres, Reds and Marlins many pitchers benefitted. I saw the positive effect of his work initially in 1972 with pitchers Paul Splittorff, Steve Busby, Al Fitzmorris, Dennis Leonard, Mark Littell and others; later with Eric Show, Greg Booker, Ed Whitson, and others in the early 1980s when I was General Manager of the San Diego Padres; then Pete Harnisch, Danny Graves, Scott Williamson and others with the Cincinnati Reds.

Bill was right, "Pitch command is all about focus. Every action should begin with what the pitcher focus upon and should end with what the pitcher focuses upon." When done properly their execution was great. When done improperly their poor execution hurt our team.

Bill taught and trained my pitchers with the "right stuff." I know he certainly got me thinking about things differently, literally seeing the game from a different viewpoint, and it had a positive impact on my managing. I learned that hitting, fielding, base running was first and foremost a "visually guided task." Through his help, I worked with my players to encourage they had better discipline of their eyes and their vision.

I am quite sure as a result of this training my young players learned the game more rapidly. They were able to be exposed to new information and then transfer into action on the field. Without question, they became better defensive players and most improved their hitting.

Prior to 1972, I don't recall anyone in baseball ever talk about visual thinking, but he showed our pitchers how to do it. Back in those days, no one thought anyone could improve their concentration, but he certainly trained our players in ways that improved their focus. To my knowledge, he was the first in baseball to emphasize that visual thinking was the way athletes and managers thought. He encouraged my players to picture their actions in advance and to focus on seeing the target and nothing else. Visual thinking and picturing were rather strange words, but it worked.

I recommended Bill to my team owners Ewing Kauffman, Charley Finley, Ray Kroc and Marge Schott to retain him and have set on the bench, but it never worked out. I doubt Bill would have taken the job anyway, but I know he would have helped us a lot.

Bill has spent his life studying champions, determined to find those qualities and common ingredients that made them champions. Through forty years of working with leading Olympic and professional athletes, he discovered, developed and refined his program to help players and coaches achieve consistent top performance. I think he has a lot of answers.

Now, after my sixty years in the game, I have been exposed to just about every type of person, every idea, and every coaching style and method. I've also had every type of player. I've had super intelligent and super dumb players.

Bill helped me understand the importance of foundational skills that underlie performance. If a guy can't focus, perhaps he has an unusually short attention span, he isn't going to prepare as well as he should.

My pitchers gained a broad understanding of how to

handle the many challenges of playing the game. They learned how to rivet their concentration on the task at hand, whatever it was.

This level of focus helped them overcome distractions. It is easy to get distracted playing baseball. But the players Bill worked with rarely were distracted because they learned how to determine where their focus needed to be and learned how rivets their full attention on their primary task of the moment.

As a result of what he taught many of my players was to step on the mound, on every pitch, be free of thought, fully confident and focus on their target.

If you need consistency, if you want to pitch to your potential all the time, if you want to eliminate mental mistakes, I think you must read and subsequently, study what Dr. Bill Harrison has for you in his Slow The Game Down program.

SECTION I:

Putting a Visual and Brain-Based Approach into Action

Most everyone will agree that pitching is not just physical, but is highly mental. In fact, most will agree that pitching is highly visual. However, nearly all effort to become a better pitcher is a physical-based effort.

Part of this is because though the mental and visual sides of pitching are recognized as important, very few know what to do in order to become more effective with those two critical aspects.

The following chapters will familiarize you with what a number of major league pitchers have done, some of their trials and tribulations and the efforts they made to improve their pitching skills.

Within these chapters many ideas are embedded that upon discovery and use will likely help you become more effective, more consistent and be able to maintain your pitch command.

.

Introduction

The Highest of Highs and the Lowest of Lows

If you are going to be a pitcher you are going to understand that pitching provides a test of your intention, your steadiness of focus, and the discipline in which you prepare for each pitch! And the bottom line is you are always challenged to perform at your very best, as pitching gives you immediate rewards and punishments. The punishment can be very painful, at least emotionally. Yet, the rewards can be great. You'll learn that consistently effective pitch command is more dependent upon Focus Acuteness than solely on physical superiority. Focus failure directly results in poor pitch command, pitches that are hittable or that are balls. Pitchers' mistakes are very common, and pitchers that don't possess focus acuteness invariably exhibit focus failure. Major league hitters feast on them. Pitchers are trained in everything, with very advanced biomechanics, strength and conditioning programs and are provided great analytics in regards to the strengths and weaknesses of the hitters they face. But few pitchers are trained on how to develop "Focus Acuteness," they are just expected to have it. And they are expected to have it from their first pitch in the game to the last pitch of the game. And if they don't have it they spend a lot of time sitting in the bullpen and tend to start thinking about another career. Pitch command is the greatest of a pitcher's talents and without focus acuteness, they don't have a chance of having it. Your pitch command will improve as you spend the time to develop and use a Personal Focusing Plan to help you persevere and overcome adversity, to conquer pressure and unexpected events, to be totally self-reliant and be able to overcome the fears of failure or success.

This book is about performing as it is about achieving your goals. We offer our insights, observations, and assumptions about how you can positively express your talents. It is not intended to be the ultimate answer as it is designed to get you to think and discuss with others how you can best express your talent on the mound.

The stories in this book include a young pitcher going from Low-A ball to the Major Leagues in less than one year — Mark Littell; a historical .500 pitcher who became the Kansas City Royals first 20 game winner and an early inductee to the Kansas City Royals Hall of Fame — Paul Splittorff; a veteran ace who was a World Series Ace who suddenly lost total pitch command — Steve Blass; an amazing Cy Young and World Series MVP who pitched 59 consecutive scoreless innings — Orel Hershiser; a 355 game winner along with 4 Cy Young Awards and a 2014 inductee to Baseball's Hall of Fame — Greg Maddux; stories about a young Chicago Cubs and a veteran Atlanta Braves pitching staffs; a big career U-turn by a young struggling major league pitcher — Jason Johnson; and a phenomenal career turnabout by a veteran — Pete Harnisch.

Though there are current professional and major league pitchers who have been trained in this unique approach and each has equally interesting stories, they are not included since they are still competing.

Please keep in mind the majority of the ideas presented were first introduced to baseball in the 1970's at the Kansas City Royals Baseball Academy. They've stood the test of time. It's possible you have heard some of the concepts or read their interpretation in books written by others who first learned them in seminars and workshops we presented. Hopefully, this book will strengthen your understanding of where these ideas came from, why you can benefit and how you can get the maximum out of your talent.

If you are like most pitchers, your pitching performance can have the sharp ups and down of a roller coaster. Do you experience the highest of highs occasionally and then the lowest of lows much too often? This book promises to guide you in reaching your highs much more often while reducing your lows.

If you want to be a pitcher, you must understand that pitching provides a test of your intention, your steadiness of focus, and the discipline in which you prepare for each pitch! And the bottom line is you are always challenged to perform at your very best, as the game gives you immediate rewards and punishments. The punishment is often very painful, at least emotionally. Yet, the rewards can be great.

Pitchers are truly unique individuals. Pitchers come in all sizes, personalities and demeanors, and the best aren't necessarily the biggest or strongest. They are all different, but their common denominator is that they have to be great athletes. Part of being a great athlete is having a great mental approach to pitching.

Even if the same size or similar pitching mechanics, their brains function differently. Pitching coaches are rightfully highly admired for their ability to coach these distinctly different individuals.

There are a lot of unfounded theories and hypotheses about what it takes to be an effective pitcher. Some are very helpful. Others are absolutely nuts.

Pitching is a highly unique human experience. If you haven't been a pitcher, you can be an observer, but never actually understand what it is like to pitch.

Greg Maddux, Randy Johnson, Danny Graves, Nolan Ryan, Rick Reuschel, Jim Kaat, John Smoltz, Pedro Martinez,

Barry Zito and Satchel Paige were not the same. But they each exhibited great pitching talent.

My observation is their most common trait was their "Focus Acuteness," when they were on the mound. These guys could get "locked and loaded" and remain "locked." Pitchers with focus acuteness pitch while making fewer mistakes.

Pitching is very demanding as it requires the ability to persevere and overcome adversity, to conquer pressure and unexpected events, to be totally self-reliant and be able to overcome the fears of failure or success. And often these capabilities are required despite discomfort, fatigue, emotions, pain and unexpected change.

Being acutely focused on every pitch, for even one inning is a challenge. Focusing for nine innings is quite a feat. It is not easy. Few can do it. Those that do enjoy a great journey and many get handsomely compensated.

Throughout baseball the common complaint of pitching coaches is their pitchers cannot consistently command their fastball. These coaches see a lack of pitcher's ability to repeat their delivery. They help these pitchers work hard on their pitching mechanics. After all, loss of pitching command is preceded by a pitch mechanics breakdown. However, the decline in pitch mechanics is often preceded by focus failure.

The question that needs to be considered is "Is a loss of pitch command due to lack of physical mechanics or is it a result of focus failure?"

You be the judge. But before you make that decision, consider the consistency of your focus as you do your work in the bullpen. Do you always have focus acuteness, locked into the zone when you pitch in the bullpen? Or are you always searching, making an adjustment, chasing a fleeting feeling?

Pitchers that don't possess focus acuteness invariably

exhibit focus failure. Focus failure directly results in poor pitch command, pitches that are hittable or walks. Focus failure always results in pitcher's mistakes. Pitchers' mistakes are very common. Major league hitters feast on them.

Pitchers are trained in everything, with very advanced biomechanics and strength and conditioning programs. But few are trained on how to develop "Focus Acuteness." They are just expected to have it. And they are expected to have it from their first pitch in the game to the last pitch of the game. And if they don't they spend a lot of time sitting in the bullpen and perhaps should start looking for another career.

We suggest consistently effective pitching is more dependent upon Focus Acuteness than physical superiority. Pitch command is the greatest of a pitcher's talents and without focus acuteness, they don't have a chance of having pitch command.

To advance as a pitcher, you must continue to learn. You are going to learn something about learning. You have to be yourself. But you can learn from others.

You are going to learn about the use of your own Personal Focusing Plan that will help you to gain control of your focus acuteness with a consistent progression of focus. It will help you continue pitching effectively and it will help you minimize and recover rapidly from your down cycles.

You will learn how to consistently repeat a focus progression, despite distractions, frustration, bad calls, etc. A good plan will help you perform at a critical moment, notwithstanding the speed of the action, rapid change, distractions, stress, and surprises. Proper use will positively impact your ability to make your pitch decision, to remain calm and to as you see and think clearly under all circumstances. Your Personal Focusing Plan will allow you to act, not react and to control your response to any challenge. It will give you total focus while you are pitching and enable you to learn from what you do. By always using your plan, you will enjoy higher self-confidence.

Expected benefits from your Personal Focusing Plan are expected to include:

- Helping you stay focused with a consistent progression of focus from the moment you step on the rubber until the moment you release of the ball from your fingertips. You will learn how to repeat this focus sequence despite frustration, bad calls, bad defense, rapid change, distractions, stress, and surprises.

- Helping you persevere and overcome adversity, to conquer pressure and unexpected events, to be totally self-reliant and be able to overcome the fears of failure or success.

- Helping your ability to make quality decisions, to remain calm, perform at a critical moment as you see and think clearly under all circumstances.

- Helping you develop superior focus so your body will remain relaxed, maintain a sense of rhythm, and keep your fine muscle coordination as you lock on a specific target.

- Helping you increase the amount of time you pitch "In the Zone."You will gain an ability to recover rapidly when out of the zone and know how to get back to your high level of performance.

- Helping you to thoroughly prepare visually and mentally so that you can concentrate on one or more key mechanics in the bullpen. You will then be able to shift to a state of mind on the mound that is 100% focused on throwing a high-quality pitch through a specific target.

- Putting you in control and allows you to have a composed, clearheaded response to varying demands that occur when you pitch. It removes the uncomfortable and sometimes disastrous position of being at the mercy of what is happening around you.

- Helping you learn how to control your concentration so you have the ability to stay consistently focused one pitch at a time.

"How2Focus: The Pitcher's Zone" is about maximizing your talent as a pitcher so you can achieve focus acuteness that will lead you to a high-quality performance. Therefore, it is about success because success is the byproduct of your performance. Success is the natural outcome of putting your talents and abilities to work for you. Success is what you get when you consistently perform well on the mound.

We offer our insights, observations, and assumptions about how you can positively express your talents. It is not intended to be the ultimate answer as it is designed to get you to think and perhaps discuss with others how you can best express your talent on the mound.

We have written this book not purely as an instructional book but in a unique narrative format. Our hope is that you will gain some unique perspectives, practical applications, and strategies from formerly successful, well-known pitchers that you can you use as a pitcher or as a coach helping pitchers.

The intent of each story is for you to gain insights and for you to learn something that can be valuable to your pitching efforts. The purpose of the stories in this book is so you can learn the methods, strategies, and techniques used by various well-known pitchers. The goal is for you to be able to incorporate insights from these stories to help you achieve your objectives and help you overcome your challenges.

We recommend you read this book multiple times as you will get out of it what you bring to it. There are many insights embedded within the various stories. If you have pitched very little, you may not recognize many of those insights. As you become a more experienced pitcher, those ideas will likely pop out, and many will be insights you will want to use.

We put this information forward to you, then, in the spirit of sharing the unique ideas we have learned over the last forty years. Why do we think you will benefit? The most powerful human skills are intention and attention followed by a proactive action are achievable by all pitchers, no matter your physical strength or your experience level.

So let's go forward and look at considerations that will help you express your talent.

Chapter 1

Pitching Brilliance as Expressed by Great Pitch Command

Emphasis is placed on how you can succeed as a pitcher without having a 100 mph fastball, a devastating changeup, or the world's best breaking pitch. You'll discover that military sniper and marksman-like focus is a more acute focus and one in which you sense you are more riveted to attending to a specific feeling, a specific sound, a specific thought or a specific visual target. You'll also learn that the most powerful pitcher's skills are intention and attention followed by a proactive action are achievable by all pitchers, no matter your physical strength or your experience level. Emphasis is placed on becoming a pitcher with brilliance in the ability to read a hitter's actions. You can then pitch what hitters aren't looking for as you change locations, in and out, with varying speeds while keeping one pitch ahead of each hitter faced. You also gain insights into the importance of pitch command, how to achieve it, and how to reduce pitch mistake. You will be encouraged to use your eyes and "focus first." You will gain an understanding that having excellent pitch command may be one of the toughest things to do in sports. But you also gain an understanding that focus acuteness precedes pitch command and pitching brilliance.

Current MLB aces Zach Greinke, Clayton Kershaw, Madison Bumgarner, David Price, Mark Buehrle, and former pitchers Greg Maddux, Jamie Moyer, Tommy John, Tom Glavine, Al Leiter, Frank Tanana, Jim Kaat, Pedro Martinez, Barry Zito and old-time greats Whitey Ford and Satchel Paige were and are among many very successful pitchers that have had great pitch command.

These great pitchers exhibited pitching brilliance. In fact, these pitchers were and are amazing marksmen. When they were on their game, they rarely missed their mark.

They mastered the ability to pitch "well-located" pitches. And you can too!

Unlike flame throwers, most of these pitch command specialists did not have an exceptional gun that could produce a super high-velocity bullet. After all, not every pitcher can pitch a 100 mph fastball. Though an explosive fastball is exciting, the most important pitching skills, pitching brilliance and subsequent pitch command, is achievable by all.

They succeeded on consistent pitch command resulting in pitching brilliance. They could read the hitter's actions and then pitch what the hitter wasn't looking for as they changed locations, in and out, and changed speeds.

Pitch command is the ability to locate a pitch whenever you need to, wherever you need to. It is a byproduct of focus acuteness.

Despite all their great training, most modern Major League pitchers do not have very good pitch command. And as you go down the pyramid from AAA to Rookie Ball to Colleges to High School pitch command is even rarer.

Many pitchers have a great physical appearance. They work hard on improving their mechanics. They exhibit potential in the bullpen and show flashes of it in games.

However, no matter how great one's pitching potential

appears to be, the limiting factor is focus failure and resultant and loss of consistent pitch command. The resultant is pitch mistakes and hitters hit pitcher's mistakes.

According to Kenny Kendrena of Inside Edge, a company that specializes in statistics for professional baseball teams, the results from scouting all 2014 major league baseball games reveals that "major league pitchers only hit their intended target 24 percent of the time."

Inside Edge defines pitch command as either the catcher's glove didn't move or it was within one baseball width from the glove. That's a large target, approximately 15 by 18 inches wide. That huge target was hit only 24 percent of the time by major league pitchers. How about the accuracy of minor league, college, high school, and youth ball pitchers? 24% accuracy would not win many dart games. Lousy free throw shooters hit greater than 24%

With 24 percent accuracy, a military sniper would have to turn in his rifle and look for a different job. Marksman in the various shooting sports like skeet and trap expect to hit their target 98-99% of the time. Of course, they are totally focused on 100% success and are bummed if they miss a target once or twice.

The major league average of hitting the target 24% of the time is the average, most of the guys making the big bucks are much better. Great pitch command leads to long careers.

Pitchers who have long careers are much like marksmen. They each know where to look, when to look and how to look.

According to the *U.S. Navy SEAL Sniper Training Program,* "The shooter must know how to use their eyes."

Marksmen have to be able to "well-locate" their bullets just like pitchers have to be able to "well-locate" their pitches.

It is interesting that a trained, military sniper will hit their target with consistent precision one mile away, but pitchers fail over and over again at hitting their mark from 60 feet 6 inches?

Snipers and competitive marksmen have superior focus. Average focus doesn't get it done in marksmanship or pitching. Perhaps pitchers need to become more like a military or competitive marksmen. How does a marksman focus so well?

You can learn from marksmen and successful pitcher's keys that will help you achieve your goals.

Focus acuteness as a result of identification and commitment to a specific task at hand and subsequently following a sequence of visual focus progression repeatedly. The ideal task at hand is one of pitching a quality pitch to a specific target. It occurs when you follow your eyes and allow your eyes lead your brain and your body.

A military sniper described his acute focus as, "If you're shooting from 700 yards, you go down the scope, you become the tip of the bullet, and you project yourself those 700 yards. You're there."

I expect Greg Maddux, John Smoltz, Orel Hershiser and others would say, "Yes, I became the front of the ball and I actually rode it 60 feet, 6 inches through my specific target. I was there."

With that kind of acute focus, you don't feel your body, you don't think about anything, and you don't hear anything. It is just like Kevin Costner said in "For the Love of the Game" you "Clear the mechanism" or perhaps better said "As a result of your focus of the mechanism has been cleared." All you focus is on your specific target. Wouldn't that be great if you could do that when you were on the mound? Well, you can.

Hall of Fame pitcher Greg Maddux once told me "Despite the chaos of the game the focus acuteness required is similar to ratcheting down and down into a tiny point of detailed clarity, frequently the webbing on the catcher's glove.."

He went on to say, "After the pitch is released, you go with it, you become the front of the ball, you project yourself sixty feet and six inches. You're there when the ball pops the catcher's glove."

He thought for a moment and then said, "Sometimes you have to do it with fifty to sixty thousand people yelling and screaming. It's amazing, but you don't hear a thing."

Marksmen do it all the time. High-powered rifles are incredibly loud. They can be deafening. But the sniper has shot in war zones without muffling devices or earplugs. And a strange thing happens. "I don't hear the blast," a sniper says. "I don't hear anything."

Similarly, in baseball, when pitchers are locked in on pitching they "Don't hear anything." Again, much like the acutely focused sniper.

A marksman-like focus is a more detailed focus and one in which we sense we are more riveted to attending to our specific target.

In the military, a sniper likely is exhausted from the demanding conditions he has had to endure. He has all the reasons in the world to be overcome by fear. But he knows he has a particular task at hand and focuses one hundred percent of his capability of successfully achieving that task. He learns to trust his ability and let it happen.

"With a total focus on my task at hand, I was never aware of being fatigued," added the sniper.

Furthermore, with total focus on the task at hand, successful pitchers are much more accurate with their pitches.

An eleven-year major league veteran pitcher Rick Langford is now a pitching coach for the Toronto Blue Jays. Rich agreed with the 24% figure but said, "The consistently effective pitchers like the great Roy Halliday would hit his target 75-80% of the time."

Randy St. Claire, Blue Jays AAA pitching coach and former major league pitching coach, told me, "Major League pitchers would be very successful if they would just execute a well-located fastball."

"I believe the most successful pitchers that pitch a long period, pitch with their fastball first, and then everything plays off of that," Langford said. "I think the fastball pitchers with command and aggressiveness pitch deeper into games. That's why those are the guys that are in the seventh and eighth inning with decent pitch counts."

San Francisco Giants hitting coach Hensley "Bam-Bam" Meulens told me, "A well-located fastball is still the hardest pitch to hit."

You can't locate a pitch, have pitch command or exhibit pitching brilliance without focus acuteness. And you can't have focus acuteness if you are lost in thought, worrying about your body or pitching unaware of what you see.

Pitching talent is highly physical. But unless you have that 98-100 mph bullet, your success may be dependent upon you being a competitor with the focus of a marksman. And with that acute focus, you can be very successful.

"I would rather have a pitcher who tops out at 85 mph who has high pitch command than a pitcher who can throw the 98-100 mph bullet but doesn't know where it is going, " said veteran major league manager Jack McKeon.

Many pitchers find they have to make a change in their approach. "Reaching back and getting a little extra" is not a very useful strategy, other than possibly for a young closer with that 100 mph bullet.

After all flame throwers rarely remain flame throwers. The cumulative effect of pitching tens of thousands of pitches often takes their toll. Even the game's most naturally gifted hurlers must adapt their approach. Some pitchers transform from a kid who pumps upper-90s gas to a veteran who still stuns hitters with a sick changeup. Some flamethrowers learned to compensate for a decline in velocity by becoming a strike zone marksman. Other flame throwers reduce their use of their fastball. Instead, they pitch effectively with cutters or a devastating change-up. But if they do, still have to express a high-quality focus and an ability to hit their targets.

Some pitchers are effective in developing a new repertoire of off-speed pitches, but they never develop command. Without location, their off-speed come across to hitters as mistakes. The pitches stay elevated and break only slightly. And major league hitters' feast on pitcher's mistakes.

"Unless you can throw your fastball where you want it and when you want it, the other pitches almost become moot," Pitching Coach St. Claire said. "And if you choose to throw those other pitches all the time, you're probably going to get hurt."

To make that kind of alteration and be effective, a pitcher has to have acute focus. Pitching coaches do a great job of teaching and training the best and safest pitching mechanics. But if you are going to have pitch command with those improved mechanics, you must have the ability or learn how to focus. Without high-quality focus, you are not going to have pitch command. Without high-quality focus, you are going to throw, not pitch, too many mistakes.

Physical stature and talent potential alone does not guarantee success! Any consistently successful pitcher will tell you that high confidence, focus, composure, and mental toughness leads them to victory.

Pitching starts with a specific intent. What is your intention prior to a pitch? How good is your attention at the moment of you released the pitch you intended? Can you maintain the same intent throughout the game no matter what the game situations you are facing?

Focusing is not easy. If you're like most people, you cannot stay in the moment for much more than a few seconds. Then your brain drifts off. But you can overcome that tendency. The more you challenge your brain, the easier it'll be for you to get into the flow that leads to the zone. You must learn to seize the moment.

Are your actions controlled? Reactive action, reactions, can be exceptionally good, but can also be awful, because there is no element of control. Reactive performance leads to inconsistency. Proactive performance is an action that has an element of control. Proactive performance results in consistency.

Once you learn to do what the various pitchers in this book did, you are going to be able to have great control of your intention and desired control of your attention. This skill may be more important than your physical skills, and will aid in your control of whatever physical skills you possess.

Reflect on the state of mind you had when others said you were "Out of your mind." Were you thinking about whether you could pitch the ball? Were you thinking at all?

Consider all the phrases commonly used to describe a pitcher at his best: "He's out of his mind," "He's pitching over his head," "He's got ice water in his veins," "He's unconscious," or "He doesn't know what he is doing."

Are you that guy? Would you like to be the pitcher that others describe like that?

Great pitch command is not easy considering fatigue, distractions, and various game pressure. In fact, having great pitch command may be one of the toughest things to do in sports

Ted Williams, arguably the greatest baseball hitter of all-time, once said, "I think without question the hardest single thing to do in sport is to hit a baseball." Williams was the last major league player to hit .400 for an entire season, and that was back in 1941.

That question, in a nutshell: What's the hardest thing to do in baseball?

"I'd have to say throwing the ball where you want to throw it. That's pretty dang hard, "said former Chicago Cubs and New York Mets pitcher Turk Wendell.

"The ability to throw the ball where you want it time after time is the hardest thing to do in baseball," Danny Graves told me. "Above all, it's a matter of focus."

"It's a relatively simple task that you're doing. You're trying to throw a ball into a glove," Graves said. "But there are so many other things going on in your head. Sometimes there's other stuff going on around you, and just staying on what you're doing, for me in the past, has been the hardest thing. I think it always comes down to focusing on what you're doing on every single pitch of every game."

Mike Sweeney, a retired player and a former catcher, sympathizes and says, "It is amazingly difficult for pitchers to stay focused pitch after pitch, inning after inning. Inevitably they start making mistakes. I would think it is tougher to do than to have consistently productive at-bats."

If things aren't going well, perhaps you should consider a different perspective to solving some of your current challenges. A greater emphasis on the visual and mental side of your game may be just what you need.

Sometimes your odds of change can appear insurmountable, just like eating an elephant. Of course, to eat an elephant, it can be done, but you must eat one spoonful at a time. Of course, it will take a lot of time and lots of effort!

The proper use of the eyes to guide brain-based visual focus is no doubt a key in achieving acute focus, combatting focus failure, and in the case of a pitcher developing and maintaining pitch command.

How2Focus: **The Pitchers Zone**

Chapter 2

MARK LITTELL

How Mark Became a Strike Zone Marksman

In this chapter, you will learn about how a young 19-year-old pitcher went from being a .500 pitcher in low A Ball to the Major Leagues in only 9 months. You will gain insights on how he used his eyes to guide his brain, pictured and felt his actions in advance and incorporated multiple viewpoints so that he could separate himself from the other 75 pitchers who also wanted to pitch in the major leagues. You will learn you can, as Mark did, commit to one specific task at hand. You will learn what it is he did, including how his pre-pitch, pre-bullpen and pre-game preparation was taken to a higher level. In this chapter, you will learn how Mark Littell was the first pitcher to be trained how to use visual thinking and fine centering to guide his actions on the mound. You'll also learned how he used an effective method to clear his mind from extraneous, unrelated thoughts. You'll gain perspective that you can only control your approach since you can't control your results. You will gain insights on why once you commit to focusing on your task at hand you will control yourself, which is all you can control.

Mark Littell was in a group of about thirty pitchers when I introduced my training program to the Kansas City Royals minor league pitchers and staff at their Fall Instructional League in 1992. The introduction included giving them ideas on how to develop focus acuteness. I made an emphasis on how centering was the key to having focus. I told the group centering is an active effort of directing your energy to a target to process relevant, available information. It isn't about aiming your eyes. It isn't about blocking things out. Centering is about actively processing the available and relevant information radiating from the target that is part of your task at hand. It's a proactive action that you can direct and control and it produces a focused feeling like all of your energy is directed toward your intended target.

I recall our initial face to face meeting occurred after dinner in the complex cafeteria. Mark, a strong looking young man from Gideon, Missouri came over to the table I was sitting. His teammates knew him as "Country." He had a great response to our initial training sessions.

His manager at Waterloo in 1972, Steve Boros had already talked to me about Mark. Steve loved Mark, but he said it was difficult to keep him "corralled." Country had a live fastball, but his pitch command was severely lacking, particularly when the game was on the line.

A very friendly young man and, opened up a conversation. In fact, he had a very infectious charisma.

"Doc," he looked at me in a serious manner, "I think you have given me some vital answers on the mental side of the game."

He went on, "ideas are really working for me. I went out the next day after our meeting, yesterday and threw in the bullpen. Once I fine centered on the target, my pitch command was much better."

"Do you think you can use that Mark?" I did not think I knew him well enough to call him by his nickname which was "Country."

"Absolutely. I'd have to be a fool not to," he quickly responded. "It is a bit of an out-of-the-body experience, and it feels good."

"I'm glad it is making sense to you."

"I think most everything you said the other night was directed at me. I felt like you were talking directly to me. It made a lot of sense," he said.

"How's that, Mark?" I asked.

Mark added, "I think I have a pretty live fastball, but despite that, I really didn't have a very good year at Waterloo. I was 10-9, but I didn't pitch very well."

"What happened in Waterloo?" I probed.

"I just couldn't throw strikes when I needed to. I pitched okay at times, but whenever I got in trouble things just got worse and worse."

"Mark, when you didn't have pitch command, what did you do to try to get it back," I probed further.

He thought for a few moments and then said, "Well, I went through every mechanical solution I could think of or get from the coaches."

"Did it work?" I asked.

"Hell no, most of the time it just made me worse," he exclaimed.

"What else bothered you at Waterloo?" I further asked.

"Well, sometimes I thought I had pretty good stuff, but the opposing hitters were squaring even my good stuff. Heck sometimes they were hitting my breaking pitches," he offered.

"So what did you attempt to do about it?" I quizzed.

"Most of the time, I tried to throw my fastball harder. And I tried to get my breaking pitch to break more."

"Did that work?" I inquired.

"No, not at all. It seemed the harder I tried to throw, the harder they hit me," he sighed.

"And how about your breaking pitch," I asked. "Did it get better?"

"No, not at all. The more I tried to think about throwing it, the worse the pitch was."

"So do you think the solution to your struggle was all physical?"

"No, now that I have heard you talk, I'm sure my solution has to be using my eyes to get my visual focus correct."

We talked for a while, and I asked when his next bullpen was. "I would like to see you throw a few pitches. Can I join you on your next bullpen session?" The good natured young man was agreeable.

In those days, there was not always a pitching coach when a pitcher threw in the bullpen. This day it was just Mark and Manager Steve Boros who agreed to catch him, so I was able to talk freely to him.

After he had warmed up, I could see he had a good fastball. I said, "Mark, in addition to your heater, what pitch you want to get greater command?"

He said, "My slider, I need that pitch to complement my heater."

"Okay, now to help you fine center on your intended target, let's do something that will help you fine center on your target."

"What's that?" he asked.

"Mark, I want you to attempt to see the last 10-15 feet of your pitch before you pitch it."

So on that fall September day in Sarasota, I asked him to look out at his catcher and asked him to picture a quality slider painting the black on the outside of the strike zone."

"So, you are asking me to imagine a high quality pitch?" he asked. Before I could answer, he said, "Sure, I think I can do that," and he proceeded to look toward the catcher.

After he had done it, I asked, "Could you throw that pitch?"

"Sure, I think I can," he responded.

"Okay, picture and feel yourself doing it, then center on your desired target and let it go."

He threw a great slider. It was arguably a major league slider. The catcher responded affirmatively. Mark had experienced a teachable moment.

"That was the best slider I have ever thrown," he exclaimed. He was obviously happy with that result. Of course, it was only one pitch. The key was to be able to repeat it.

As he threw various pitches, I asked him to take the same approach. From then forward, he had much better command of his pitches.

I had asked him to do it with a pitch that he rarely threw effectively and he was shocked. All of a sudden he had great command of a slider, a pitch that until now was somewhat non-existent for Mark.

He was obviously pleased. Rather excitedly he said, "All last season at Waterloo I was never that focused on my target. I was always aware of my push-off, my release and my follow through. My pitching motion never felt this good!"

Steve Boros said, "In all my years of baseball I have never heard of a pitcher being instructed on how to visualize a pitch prior to pitching it. It makes a lot of sense to me."

Little did Mark or I know that day in Sarasota was the start of a great year at Omaha in AAA. From the low-A Midwest League to AAA Omaha was a major jump. More remarkably he pitched in the major leagues by June. All of that occurred in less than one year from that 1972 Fall Instruction day in Sarasota when we first met.

In the 1973 spring training, he was so effective in centering on throwing a quality pitch through a target he asked, "What more can I do?" Mark was a starter at the minor level and incorporated his fastball, change-up, and slider as his arsenal.

I said, "Well let's think about you are going to tend to pitch in games the way you practice. So tell me what do you do to get ready to throw in the bullpen?"

"I always make sure I am physically warmed up. If not, I jog a bit. I also use Pee Wee Bourette's stretch program and stretch out all my muscles. After that I am ready to go," said Mark.

I paused and looked him in the eye, "Well, Mark consider this. Are you really prepared to go? Are you in touch with your rhythm? Do you have a sense of the right feel of each pitch as it comes out of your hand? Do you know what part of your pitch mechanics you need to work on?"

"No, not really. I usually try to gain my rhythm and feel as I throw in the bullpen?" he responded.

"Do you always find them?" I pressed.

"Well, no. Not really. I often don't get a good sense of rhythm when I throw in the pen," he observed.

"Here's something consider. 15-20 minutes before you go to the pen, sit down and look out about sixty feet at a make believe catcher." I paused, recognizing this was starting to sound a little strange.

I then added, "From there, feel your complete pitching motion produce a high quality pitch. Feel the ball release from your fingertips and see it bust the catcher's glove as it has good life."

I paused so he could think and added, "You might want to see and feel ten different quality fastballs, down around the catcher's knees. Give it a try."

Mark proceeds and after a minute or two, looked at me and didn't say anything.

"How was that?" I asked.

"Good, I like it," he quickly responded.

"So let's do it again, but I want you to remember how it is to get the catcher's sign, feel the flow of energy through your body whether you are in the windup or stretch, feel the release of a great fastball. Then see the last fifteen or so of the trajectory of the pitch and it's attacking the glove."

Mark puts it into action.

"How was that?" I asked.

"Great. This feels good. I do have a sense of my rhythm, as you say my flow of energy, and the ball felt great coming out of my hand and the pitch looked great over the last fifteen feet."

"So Mark not only can you do that before going to the pen, but you can also do it with your second and third pitches. Let's try it again with your change-up. Remember to feel that energy building up in your body as you go through your stretch or windup as well as the proper release. Then see the last fifteen feet of the pitch as it slows down and breaks downward."

I could see Mark get into it. His eyes were steady, and he had the appearance of being locked.

When he finished, I asked, "How do you feel now."

"Doc, this is amazing. I feel just like I do when I get into the zone."

"If you were going to go to the bullpen and throw on an off day or prior to a game, do you think this might help?" I inquired.

"Without a question. I'm going to do it." And he trotted out to the field and joined in the pre-practice stretching exercises.

On another day in early spring training, Mark and I set down for lunch and discussed several things.

"Mark," knowing that he was doing well, "How are things?"

"Going great," He said. "I am just focused on my task of throwing a quality pitch through a specific target."

"I want you to consider adding another component to your pregame preparation," I suggested.

"How's that?"

"Before your next start, perhaps about thirty minutes before going to the bullpen to get ready for the game, I want you to sit down on a stool and about sixty feet away." I could tell he was listening.

"Now, initially look at yourself on the mound. Look at yourself as if you were the hitter. See yourself in the uniform you will wear tomorrow." I paused. "And then see yourself pitching a high-quality pitch to a specific target, actually a great fastball, and notice your demeanor, rhythm, tempo and, of course, the complete throwing action including your follow through."

I could see that Mark was already doing it, even though he was standing up.

"After seeing the same great actions two to three times, now let's look at the same throwing action from three or four different directions. For example, see yourself pitching as if you were watching from the third base coaching box." I paused and waited.

I added, "Now, see the same pitching action, same demeanor, same rhythm and timing, from the first base coaching box."

He was into it. I then said, "So now, let's see the same pitching action from a centerfield camera point of view."

I waited another moment and said, "Now this one will seem a little strange, but let's do the same exact thing from the view of a helicopter. Yes, imagine a helicopter hovering over the field, looking down and seeing you from directly above."

"So now, you have done that, let's now see and feel from your own eyes what it is like to throw that exact same pitch. Even though, it is from your own eyes, sense the demeanor you want to have, feel the rhythm and timing, feel the energy build up in your body and the feeling of a proper release. Then see the trajectory of your pitch pounding down toward your low outside target. Then do it again."

I allowed Mark to continue and could tell he was doing it. I interrupted by saying, "How do you feel right now?"

He paused and was almost speechless, "I feel like everything is just flowing properly for me. It is just like getting into the zone."

"So Mark, how well will you pitch from a windup and execute that pitch if you were going down to the bullpen."

"Absolutely fabulous. All I would have to do is get warm, get loose, and then I will be throwing bullets," he began to smile.

"Well, you need to do the same picturing of pitching that same fastball from the stretch," I paused to make sure he was listening.

After I could tell he was thinking, I slowly added, "And then do the same, in the windup and the stretch with all of your pitches. Do the same with your slider, then with your changeup, and then with your curve ball."

"Will it wear me out?" he asked appropriately.

"Mark, that's a very good question. But, no, you'll find you are in the zone and not aware of anything other than throwing quality pitches to your specific targets."

"I'm all in!" he responded with enthusiasm.

So the next day, two days prior to his next start, Mark through in the bullpen.

Afterward, he said, "That was unbelievable. Everything was in place. My rhythm was great. The ball came out of my hand really well. I was locked. That is the best pen I have thrown in my life."

"Mark, if you use this method prior to every pen session, you are going to gain more consistency in your actions. You won't be searching as often for the feel that seems to come and go."

"But exactly how can I use this prior to a game, or in a game?" he inquired.

"I was hoping you would ask," I countered.

I advised, "Prior to going to the pen to get ready for a game, do through about ten to fifteen pitches in this same manner. Do it by observing your windup and by observing your stretch. Remember, rhythm and tempo are keys to gain the right feel."

I paused, "Knowing who your catcher is, picture him about sixty feet away. Knowing the opposing team's lineup, feel your pitching motion and then the proper release of a high-quality pitch to a target."

I paused again, "You should make a decision on your pitch, and then see and feel it, then feel your pitching motion that is doing to produce that pitch. As you feel the energy go through your body, sense it being released from your fingers to the ball and then see the pitch again as if it was even more real."

"That's a lot, but I think I can do that," he observed.

"So go through the entire lineup once, pitching three to four good pitches to each. Then go through the lineup a second time. As it may be in the 3rd or 4th inning, be in your stretch, hold a man on and then feel and see these actions once again," I advised.

"So, I know what you are going to say next," he said. "I do it again in the 6th or 7th inning when they come up a third time and the game is on the line."

"That's it, Mark." I paused and let him do some of it.

"So finally Mark, do the same in the 9th inning with the game really on the line. See and feel how you will make the proper pitch selection, feel the great rhythm and timing and then let it happen as you get the hitter out."

"I'm excited," Mark said, "I am ready to pitch. Heck, I don't pitch for a couple of days."

"So Mark, this plan takes a lot of mental energy. If you are going to use it, it is important that you relax as much as possible the day of the game. Don't waste your energy on being too wound up or too tense."

"But, Doc, I thought I was supposed to have a game face on," Mark responded.

I thought of his comment that was actually a question, "I am not sure it is really helpful to have a game face on. It's okay to laugh. Have some fun with your teammates. Just know that thirty to forty-five minutes before you go to the bullpen you are doing to put all of your attention on this pre-game preparation routine."

Mark agreed, "I like the idea of forgetting the game face. That has never worked for me. I think this will help me stay calm, and, as a result, I will be relaxed. I like the idea of saving my available energy for when I need it."

Mark had a great spring. He started out with the AA Jacksonville team and made the most of the opportunity that he was promoted to the AAA Omaha Team in that spring training of 1973.

One day late in spring training, I spoke to Mark and he

said, "Doc, I am pitching so well. It is starting to get easy."

Cautioning him I said, "Mark, it is a long season. It's great you are off to a great start, but you are going likely going to run into some unexpected challenges."

"I know," he responded.

"So Mark after you do your pregame preparation, after feeling and seeing yourself pitch a lot of great pitches to the opposition, you will have a great sense of being ready for anything ThenI want you to incorporate another step."

"Sure, what's that?" he responded. It was clear he was willing to put any good ideas into play.

I then advise, "As you feel and see your high-quality pitches, I want you to feel yourself get in the stretch and realize you have to deal with men in scoring position."

I then added, "Additionally it's helpful to sense a degree of upset for the adversity that you are experiencing. Perhaps it is bad calls by the umpire, some fielding errors or some chink hits. Without getting mad, get committed to even a greater degree on pitching a quality pitch through your intended target."

I could see he was probably wondering why I was encouraging rather adverse situations, and then I added, "Feel and see yourself get out of the jam by executing your pitches with great pitch demand."

"So what you are saying," he responded, "is that things are not always going to be rosy out there. I need to prepare myself for what I have to do when the 'crap hits the fan.'"

I chuckled at his expressions, "That's good way to think about it, Mark. Prepare by anticipating everything that could happen, not be surprised, and keep focusing your full attention on your task at hand."

"Well, I can do that," he said emphatically.

"One other thing, Mark," I said. "Every pitcher has an

inning or two where he gets out of sorts. Without a doubt when it occurs your mechanics slip. Your manager, pitching coach and probably your catcher can see your mechanics break down."

"I know," he said. "I always have to repair my mechanics. Coach Fischer and Coach Blaylock get all over me for it."

"Well, Mark, I would like for you to think of focus first and then go to a mechanical adjustment, only if necessary. If you are starting to lose it a little bit, stop take a deep breath, clear your mind, relax for a few moments and then commit to a more attentive focus on your task at hand. 99 times out of 100, you will be back in synch, and you won't have to tinker with your mechanics."

"If that works, it will be worth a ton," he remarked.

With a stern demeanor I said, "Don't worry, Mark, it will work."

He opened the season in Omaha. It was a huge jump for a 20-year-old. But he carried his spring training approach into the season.

I visited the Omaha team in early May. Mark was 4-0 at the time.

"Doc, you are Dr. Magic," Mark said, "What you have taught me has been magical."

Knowing that Mark was likely going to find some challenges as the season went along, I asked," Mark, do you ever lose your high level of focus?"

He paused and said, "Well, sometimes I start thinking too much, and I lose that edge."

"When that happens here's a suggestion that you might want to you use." I responded and then added, "And also this is something that has the great benefit of making the glove look larger and closer to you."

"What's that? Sometimes the glove does look small and

at a long distance. I don't like that," he responded.

"Mark, this is based on the fact that when you switch your eyes rapidly from one point to another, you can't process a conscious thought in your brain." I went on, "So I suggest you look at one of the catcher's knee guards and then switch your eyes quickly to the other knee guard. Repeat that for three complete cycles and then switch your eyes directly to the catcher's glove."

"So I don't have to stare at the glove?" he inquired.

"No, to the contrary. Staring results in thinking and you can lose your focus quickly," I clarified.

He thought and then said "Wow. I know I've stared too hard and lost my focus. It has happened a lot. This is really going to help!"

He then said, "There's a large herd of pitchers, probably seventy-five, in this organization who dream of pitching in the major leagues. I now think it is going to be my eyes and my brain and not just my body that will lead me to get in front of that herd."

The Royals had to call Mark up to Kansas City to pitch for the major league team. He was not part of the 40-man roster, but he was 9-1 in AAA Omaha and other teams were attempting to pick him up off of waivers.

His debut was against Baltimore and he pitched very well as he pitched 7 plus innings and gave up 2 runs. His next outing though was against the Oakland A's, this was the team of the early 70's as they won three World Series. They walloped him.

Mark today says, "The fact is, I wasn't ready to win. But I was on my way."

He went on, "I knew that I had learned from this visual program that I had found a way to separate myself from the pack of pitchers in the minor leagues who wished they would make it. But I worked hard on the right things that I knew and believed would get me back to the major leagues."

It was an incredible ascent to the show. He probably wasn't quite ready, but what a run. After all a year earlier he was struggling in low A-Ball pitching before one hundred people at times. In Kansas City and on the road, he pitched in front of thousands. It was a much different atmosphere.

After three games with the Royals, he returned to Omaha to complete the season. A .500 pitcher in low A Ball and within in one season, he ended up with a 16-6 record and a 2.51 ERA and was named the American Association's pitcher of the year at the age of 20.

We spoke the next spring training in Fort Meyers. Mark said, "When I was in AAA I was totally focused on my task at hand of pitching a quality pitch through my target. When I got called up, I got away from it and never really got it back until I returned to Omaha. I must admit I got caught up in the large crowds and all that surrounded the games."

I asked, "Mark, with the 16 games you won in the American Association what in your mind was your task at hand?

"It was just like you told me when we first met, pitch a high-quality pitch through a specific target. It was that simple. And it sure did work."

I think he knew what the next question was going to be. I asked, "So when you got into the Major Leagues what was your task at hand?"

Mark, knowing I had him, thought for a few moments and then said, "I was trying to please everyone. I just wanted to stay."

He paused and then said, "You are one hundred percent right, I got away from my task."

"Mark, you have to start thinking in terms of controlling what you can control. You can only control your approach. You can't control your results. Commit to focusing on your task at hand. In this manner, you will control yourself, which is all you can control."

Mark told me, "I used to sweat and work just 'way too hard' and learning to use my brain allowed me to work easy and work smart, as I knew what I can and also what I could not do."

At 21, Mark went through an elbow surgery after throwing close to 300 innings. Between spring training, AAA Omaha, Royals call-up, AAA Omaha, Royals September call-up, then 75 innings in Puerto Rico anybody could see that this was truly an overload. All of his real quality big league time came after the surgery.

Years later Mark told me several things about his career that were very insightful. He said, "I had two surgeries, one on my elbow, and the other on my shoulder, six years apart, and bounced back from both."

He said, "Not many people know is that I could focus on the rehab program and rebound much quicker. I went from 89-91 mph to 93-95 mph in a matter of 4 months from the surgery. What I had learned from about visual thinking, how to harness my focus points, and enhancing the power of visual thinking helped me through any physical event."

He paused and then said, "Rebounding from surgery is tough but being upbeat and knowing how to stay positive were now in my favor. I sensed I had an edge. I could actually relax that six inches from temple to temple and I knew how to get to that point and alleviate the pain and stress level to a controlled effort of all the senses."

I asked, "Please clarify that for me, Mark."

He pointed out, "In other words by having success in my pitching with visual thinking I found it a big advantage of making a comeback. Seeing myself do the little things, including my elbow and shoulder repair and myself pitching correctly, was paramount in getting me over the hump."

"Also, prior to throwing, I actively pictured my proper throwing action. Later I did a lot of mental bullpens before being able to do physical bullpens," he shared. "By doing that, long before I could physically do it, it helped me regain my pitching skills more rapidly."

"Did it really help?" I asked curiously.

"Absolutely," he said vigorously, "It made a big difference in my recovery."

I knew at that time in September 1972 I had never seen a pitcher, heard a pitcher talk about or had I asked a pitcher to do just that. But it had worked very well with the professional golfers I was working with at the time, and I thought with Mark's receptive attitude he just might very be able to do it.

As time went on, many pitchers have been quoted in the media on how they had visualized pitching well and they subsequently pitched just like they visualized.

After his career, Mark told me, "Doc, I think I was the first professional pitcher ever to utilize consciously the ability to picture or imagine a pitch before I pitched it. I know the other pitchers could see me just staring off into space. I think many of the guys in the minor leagues thought I was nuts. But they didn't make it to the show. And I sure did."

He went on, "Also, I was probably also the first pitcher to ever get instructed how to fine center on a small target and maintain it while pitching the ball through that small target. I very well was among the first pitchers to work on his balance to have a more relaxed body, and a looser arm and fingers. And I am sure I was one of the first pitchers taught how to use my eyes to clear my mind. Additionally, learning how to see my pitching action from multiple viewpoints, particularly a helicopter viewpoint, was a great benefit."

He then said, "I think what I learned from you was to 'Picture and feel doing it, and then pitch it through a specific target.' And when I was healthy it really worked. I know it took me out of a pack of seventy-five or so minor league pitchers and propelled me to nine seasons in the big leagues."

Mark Littell enjoyed a 9 year MLB pitching career. He had a lifetime ERA of 3.32 and saved 56 games from 1976 to 1981. Primarily a relief pitcher, Littell served at the Royals' closer in 1976-1977. After the 1977 season, the Royals dealt Littell, along with catcher Buck Martinez, to the Cardinals in exchange for all-star relief pitcher Al Hrabosky.

After appearing to have fully recovered from his elbow surgery, bone spurs developed in his elbow and cut his career short, and Littell retired midway through the 1982 season at the age of 29. He set the single-season record for St. Louis Cardinals relief pitcher strikeouts in any one season.

Following his pitching career, Mark has stayed in the game as a youth coach but not before coaching professionally for 18 years, spending 4 years in Australia, Puerto Rico, Dominican Republic, and Panama.

He also used his creativity to develop a unique product for all athletes—the Nutty Buddy, a protective cup that allows for greater comfort and mobility.

Chapter 3

PAUL SPLITTORFF

Prepared Like an Astronaut, Performed like a Sniper

In this chapter, you will learn how a .500 pitcher in college, in the minor leagues and his first two years in the major leagues became a 20 game winner and an all-time pitching leader for his organization. You will learn about an off the field drill he used to develop his ability to control whether he was in a broad, general focus or a narrow, specific focus. You will learn that when pitching, the flow of energy through your body is important. From the moment, you start your pitching action until the moment of release, your energy goes from static, non-moving, into a flow. You'll learn the importance of know what the proper flow of energy is and then to produce it before you pitch your pitch. You will learn how he got so focused that he was unaware of the cold weather, background sounds when he pitched. You will also learn how adversity set him back and how he managed to get back to his level of capability. You will learn how his pre-bullpen preparation method aided his consistency and effectiveness. Like Mark Littell before him, Paul implemented learned how to implement an effective Personal Focusing Plan that helped him repeat a focus sequence despite frustration, bad calls, bad defense, rapid change, distractions, stress, and unexpected surprises.

In 1972, Kansas City Royals owner, Ewing M. Kauffman, committed to the use of our training program with the team's position players. Very enthusiastic about the results, he asked us to provide a similar program for the pitching staff.

Our home for two weeks in January 1973 was the Muehlebach Hotel a historic hotel building in Downtown Kansas City that was visited by every President from Theodore Roosevelt to Ronald Reagan. It had an indoor basketball gymnasium that provided us ample training space for our training drills and meeting rooms for our consultations.

Pitchers at this special pre-season training included Bruce Dal Canton, Steve Busby, Dick Drago, Tom Murphy, Tom Burgmeier, Al Fitzmorris, Wayne Simpson, Steve Mingori, Ken Wright and Paul Splittorff.

At the Muehlbach, newly named Royals Manager Jack McKeon introduced me to Splittorff. I could tell that Jack really liked Paul as he obviously had some very likable characteristics.

Jack later told me, "I've had Paul for two years at Omaha. He has shown signs of being a very effective pitcher, but he has been 25-24 in AAA. Last year, he was 12-12 for the Royals. But I think he can be better than a .500 pitcher. He just hasn't been consistent, makes too many mistakes and likely it is his focus that is holding him back."

New Royals pitching Coach Galen Cisco added, "If Paul can learn to focus better, he will be one of our starters." Little did Jack, Galen or I suspect that Paul was going to become one of Kansas City's all-time great pitchers.

Paul was a very pleasant, calm person who didn't waste a lot of words. He fit the description of a "solid citizen." Drafted after a college career at Morningside College in Iowa, he was selected in the 25th round of the 1968 amateur draft.

I also didn't know that Paul was going to be another one of my very important laboratory subjects. From his willingness to apply and give me feedback, I gained a sense of how powerful and effective these methods would eventually be for future pitchers.

Similar to how I explained the concept of centering to Mark Littell as I had the previous fall at the Instructional League and Baseball Academy in Sarasota.

I asked, "Paul, what is your target when you pitch?"

"Well, it depends," he replied.

I explained to Paul what a fine center and that a fine, narrow center occurred when he was so attentive to a very small area that it was if nothing else existed.

I also explained that a soft center occurred when he was focused on a larger area.

I asked, "When you pitch do you have a soft visual center or a fine visual center?"

He thought for a few moments and then said, "I think when I am pitching well I am in a fine center, but too often I've allowed myself to fall into a soft center. I am sure more than half the time I am in a soft center. I see everything and my pitches tend to go all over the place. For certain I lose my pitch command when I am soft centered."

"Well, let's see if we can develop some command of that ability."

I took Paul over to a wall and showed him two Vision Performance Cross Trainer charts, we called the VPX-T

I offered, "Paul take a look at these two charts."

I then asked, "What do you see?"

"Well, I see a bunch of balls with numbers. And I see the balls surrounded by different colored triangles. I see red, blue, yellow and green triangles," he responded.

I had him turn away from the posters and asked "What kind of balls are on the chart?"

"Gosh, I don't know I saw a few baseballs, but I am not sure what the others balls exactly were."

"Take a look then," I suggested.

"Ah, there are footballs, basketballs, golf balls, soccer balls, softballs as well as the baseballs."

"Paul, we all tend to focus on what we look for. It's natural for you to see the baseballs, but notice sometimes you see something, come to a conclusion and yet there is more there."

"I see what you mean," he responded.

Then I asked, "So is there anything else you might see?"

"I don't think so."

"How about the shadow on each ball," I pointed at the chart. "See on this ball the shadow is on the top, on this one the shadow is on the left, on this one the shadow is on the right, and on this one the shadow is on the bottom."

"Wow, I had no idea. I certainly didn't see."

"This points out there is often more to see than we tend to pay attention."

"I can sure see that, no pun intended," he replied.

"Now, on this single chart there are 50 balls and each has a number one through fifty," I hesitated.

I turned him away from the chart and then said, "I want you to search the chart to find ball numbers 23, tell me what ball it is on, tell me where the shadow is located and also tell me on which side of the ball is the yellow triangle." As he thought about his assignment, I said, "And I'm going to time you with a stopwatch."

"Okay."

"Go."

I watched him start the search and could tell he was a little surprised that he couldn't readily find the 23. After twelve seconds, which seemed like a long time, he found it.

"There it is."

"What ball is it on?" I asked.

"Oh yes, that's right. It's a soccer ball."

"Anything else you want to tell me?" I further asked.

"Oh, that's right you asked about where the shadow is located. I see it now. It is on the top."

"Wasn't there something else you were to tell me?" I challenged.

"On that's right, the yellow triangle is on the bottom," he finally said. He then added, "That wasn't as easy as it would seem."

"You now have some firsthand experience with how challenging centering can be. Notice you went from a soft center to a fine center when you found the 23. But then you let it go back to a soft center and forgot all the other information I had requested you were to find. As you couldn't find the 23, you got further committing to finding it, but at the cost of remembering the other things you were supposed to do."

"It was surprisingly difficult," he mused.

"Well, we are just beginning. It's going to get a little more challenging. Are you up to it?"

"Yeah, bring it on."

I paused, "So this time, I want to know the ball, the location of the shadow, and I want you to reach out and touch the tip of the red triangle on each ball. I want you to find the 50, and then the 45, then the 40 and finally the 35. Now, before you start, I also want you to start doing jumping jacks on this mini-tramp."

He looked at me rather quizzically and then muttered to himself "Whew."

He got started and actually did surprisingly well. He

found each number, told me the ball behind each number, reported the shadow location on each ball and touched the tip of each red triangle.

When he finished, he said, "Did I get them right?"

"You sure did. Let me ask you, Paul, how was your focus while you did that drill?"

"I was locked. It was just like I am when I pitch well. I wasn't aware of anything else," he observed.

"Now we are going to do something with the charts that are a little different. Notice that each chart has 5 vertical columns and 10 rows."

"I see," he responded.

"So now I am going to tell you which column that I want you to go downward and then on the other chart I am going to tell you which column I want you to go upward. In each case when you see the ball, I want you to tell me the number you see plus 3. That is if you see an 11 you will say it is a 14. Then tell where the shadow is on the ball by jumping in the direction of the shadow. Of course, it will be easy to jump up, to the left or the right. But if the shadow is on the bottom, I want you to jump backward." I paused to see his response.

"Doc, you are working me over."

We both chuckled and I said, "Just remember to see how well you can center your attention on the proper target, get into a fine center and see the distinguishing details, and combine what you see with a simple movement."

"Okay, are you ready? If so, I want you to go downward on column 1 on the chart on the left and upward on column 10 on the chart on the right. However, I am going to spread them about fifteen feet apart, so you are going to have to include some lateral movement. Only call out the type of ball, not the number, nor tell me the shadow location."

"Doc, you are going to do me in?" he asked.

"No, you can do it."

Paul proceeded to begin moving toward the left chart, found the top ball, then moved to the right chart and found the bottom ball. He called out the correct ball until he got to the 6th ball up on the right chart. For a moment, confusion set in and I could tell he was getting a little lost. But he recovered rapidly and completed the task.

He finished and said, "Wow, what a workout. I can't believe how tough this is mentally." But he paused and then said, "But I did it."

"How focused were you?"

"I was locked in that time."

"So, Paul, do you think you could use this drill in baseball."

He thought for a few minutes and then said, "I think I would like to use it in the clubhouse before a game. Often I get too fired up, and my mind starts running all over the place. I think I could use some form of this drill just to get me locked in."

"Paul, I will give you a simple, yet challenging exercise you can use. It won't require the movement like we did here, but it will fully require you to get totally focused. As you do it, it will get your mind off of most everything.

He had great capability. I was very surprised how well he did on this simple, but very challenging drill

I was confident that if he would just learn exactly what to focus upon and when to do it, he would be very effective. I thought this is the guy I would like to have as my quarterback, my point guard, or my caddy. I also thought he ought to be one heck of a pitcher. I concluded that he was going to be much better in his future than he was in his past. Unless he were on a bad team, he should be much better than a .500 pitcher. He should be a big winner in my opinion.

"Do you think this understanding of centering will influence your pitching?" I inquired.

With a quick response, he said, "Absolutely, I see it helping me a lot."

Instructing him further I said, "Paul, you always have a choice. There are times, particularly in your bullpen work you will want to either soft or fine center in your body."

He asked, "What do you mean by either soft or fine centering in my body."

I went on, "If you soft center internally in your body you may have a sense of a part of your body or your entire pitching motion. If so, you will have a soft visual center on where you are pitching the ball. You'll have a general idea of where you want to throw it, but not a specific target."

After a pause, I then added, "An alternative would be to fine center on your foot or one of your hands throughout your motion."

Paul said, "So this would be a very specific focus?"

"Yes I pointed out that this would be a good thing when he was trying to refine a specific action, but to realize the rest of his body would likely not function fluidly and accurately. Again if you are fine centered in your body, you are going to lose most of your visual awareness on your target."

"Doc, you are suggesting that it is okay for me to center in my body for throwing in the bullpen. I am sure that is what I usually do. But should I do that in a game?" he asked.

"No, I firmly stated. "Paul. In the game, you want to learn to totally trust your body's actions and not center upon them. At the moment of release of the pitch you want to be fine centered externally on a specific target you can see."

He quickly asked, "So, is it always centering on the glove?"

I clarified by saying, "It can be just the glove. But it can be the dark area in the catcher's glove, it can be the webbing in the glove, or it can even be a scratch on a knee guard. It can even be on a small window over home plate, but that is harder to do. Remember, it is your choice. "

"I can remember times that though I wanted to center on my catcher's glove, I just couldn't get my attention out of my body. How do I handle something like that in the future?" Paul asked.

I was pleased to gain the sense that Paul was thinking about how to put these ideas into practical use.

I looked around the gym and saw an electrical outlet that we could use as a target.

"Paul come over here with me" as I walked toward a spot in the gym that was about sixty feet away from the electrical outlet."

"So standing in your windup, look at that electrical outlet, but I want you to feel how the floor feels under your feet, I want you to feel your shoulder, think about whatever you are thinking about." I let him do those things for a few moments.

"Now you are looking at the electrical outlet but are you fine centered on it?" I asked

"Not at all. I have been thinking about my feet, my shoulder, and my thoughts."

"Okay so now, I want you to recall what a good slider looks like. I also want you to remember what it feels like." I paused, "Now, I want you to feel your body the way it feels when you pitch a slider and then see what you typically see of the trajectory of the pitch going through your target. Just see what you usually see."

"Okay, that's pretty easy to do."

"So tell me, Paul, now that you have done that are you fine centered on the electrical outlet?"

"Absolutely. I'm one hundred percent locked in on it."

"Do you think you could throw that pitch and hit your target?" I asked.

"Without a question. I am sure I could."

"Paul, I want to encourage that you develop the habit of not pitching a pitch without feeling your body pitch it and see the pitch go directly to your specific target."

Paul thought for a moment "I think I've done it before an occasional pitch but not on every pitch."

"Could you do it on every pitch?" I probed.

He thought for a moment and then said, "I believe I can, but we'll have to see. I will certainly give it a try."

In spring training, a month later, Paul told me that he was going to utilize everything I taught him, but in spring training he would primarily center on his mechanics. He said he traditionally just worked on the physical part of the game in spring training so he could get in shape for the season.

One day in mid-spring training, I was watching Paul throw in the bullpen. He was struggling, particularly with his curveball and changeup.

I just watched and wasn't going to say anything unless he or pitching Coach Cisco invited me to speak.

The catcher caught a bouncing ball on his wrist and needed to take a break.

Paul looked over at me and said, "Doc, I can't get any feel for my curveball. I know it is early, but I am anxious to throw it with some effectiveness."

I asked, "What are you centering on?"

He thought for a moment and said as he moved his left hand in a curveball throwing action, "I'm trying to snap it off and get some good spin on it."

Then he said, "I just can't find the right feel for the

pitch."

"Let's try this. Step off the rubber and look midway down the catcher's left knee guard. Now, picture a tight spinning curve breaking down to that spot on the knee guard." Then I added, "Do it two or three times."

He nodded that he had done so and I asked, "What do you think?"

He said, "Interesting."

He thought further, likely repeating the picture in his mind, "I now have the feeling I have been searching for. I have a better sense of how the ball should come out of my hand. I think I can throw it now."

"So clear your mind of all of this. Now when you step back on the rubber, commit to the pitch you are going to pitch. Then reproduce the feeling in your body of pitching a quality pitch and then see the results of that feeling as the pitch travels toward home plate and through your intended target," I advised.

He stopped for a moment to think about what I said. Paul stepped on the rubber, started his motion. The pitch was perfect. Just what he wanted.

He turned and looked at me and said, "I don't know why I didn't think of that before! It's rather magical!"

"Paul if you can practice that approach on at least fifteen to twenty of your last pitches in the bullpen, then when you go into the game it will be rather automatic to do. You are going to own that magic."

"Doc, it is rather amazing. I have to admit most of my focus has been on my push off leg. Even when I was trying to get the feel for my curveball, I still had a lot of attention on my push off leg."

I didn't say anything, wanting him to keep thinking about what he was in the process of discovering.

He beamed, "I can really see the value of reproducing the complete feel and the sight of a pitch I have previously thrown effectively. That's a lot better than just thinking about my leg or my release."

I picked up on his enthusiasm, "Paul, the flow of energy is important. From the moment, you start your pitching action until the moment of release, your energy goes from static, non-moving, into a flow. It's important to know what that is and then to produce it before you pitch your pitch."

I could see him looking further as he looked out at his catcher and he then said, "After a produce the feel I can see the pitch clearly travel toward my target. I like that picture," he grinned.

His catcher got back into position, and Paul pitched a fifteen or so great pitches.

He looked over at me as he completed his workout, "Doc, I got it. This is going to work. I sense it gives me a lot of confidence."

"Paul, every athlete is always searching for the right feel," I commented.

"For sure," he agreed.

"Well, it may surprise you but the best feel comes from no specific feel at all," I paused so he could think about that one.

Paul thought about it and began to nod affirmatively, "By gosh, you are right Doc."

I then emphasized, "The best feel is a flow. It's energy flowing through your body."

It was a Eureka moment for Paul. He looked stunned but said, "I've been searching for the right feel in the wrong way. This is a phenomenal thought. I can't wait to make this change."

Paul pitched so well in the last two weeks of spring

training he was named by new manager Jack to be the starting pitcher in the opening game. It was not only the opening game of the season but the first game in the new Kansas City Royals baseball stadium. Prior to spring training veteran pitcher, Dick Drago or Steve Busby, the Royals' young star pitcher, were the most likely pitchers to be considered the ace of the team, but Paul's late spring training pitching elevated him to that spot.

A week before the end of spring training I asked him, "Tell me about your focusing plan."

I knew I had stumped him as he looked at me as if I had asked him the strangest question one could ask.

I said, "You've indicated that focus is important to you. It would seem that anything that important warrants your developing a defined plan."

"Well, when you say it in that way, I agree I should have a more definite plan," he nodded affirmatively.

I tried to impress on him the importance by saying, "Without a personal focus plan, Paul, you are just leaving everything to chance. One day you will do it one way and on another day you will likely do it differently."

I paused, in fact, you should have a personal focus plan for the days you pitch in the bullpen, in the clubhouse days that you pitch, in the bullpen as you warm up, on the mound, between hitters, between innings and in your after game review."

"Wow, that's a lot," he responded.

"Paul, you are a professional and you should always be learning but also solidifying your approach."

Paul thought about it and said, "I guess you are right. I usually focus on what my pitching coach tells me to focus on, and sometimes what I hear other pitchers talk about what they are doing."

"Do you want to be like them, or do you want to be yourself?" I inquired in a manner to get him to think.

Without giving him time to reply I added, "A good plan puts you in control and allows you to have a composed, clearheaded response to varying demands that occur when you pitch. It can provide you a simplified method for implementing and applying your skills in any and all situations. It can remove the uncomfortable and sometimes disastrous position of being at the mercy of what is happening around you."

I could see he was thinking about what I was saying, so I went on.

"Paul, furthermore the use of a plan allows you to act, not react and to control your response to any challenge. It gives you total focus while you are performing and enables you to learn from the things you do."

I halted for a moment so he could think and then added, "By always using a plan, which allows for a consistent progression of thought, you will enjoy higher self-confidence and poise. It helps you channel your energy and mobilize your resources to give your best performance under any circumstances. With a self-managed plan, you can be composed, self-confident and in control at all times."

Paul looked up, "This is making a lot of sense. Instead of leaving everything to chance I see I need to take control of what I can control."

"By following a plan you make sure that nothing is left out. Keep in mind that by following and acting according to a plan you are not limiting spontaneity or creativity, you are allowing it to happen," I further advised.

"I like the idea. I need to spend some time making myself a good plan," he said agreeably.

I further stated, "It is a dynamic guide and is not a static, fixed rulebook. It is flexible so that you can respond to changes with little effort. You will find that you can just allow your actions to happen. "

He nodded affirmatively and then asked, "Will this help me handle distractions?"

I responded, "It will help you overcome all obstacles including distractions, stress, fear and anxiety and allows you to make things happen. You will stop trying to arrive at that state and will find yourself just being there naturally. It can lower anxiety by eradicating outside stimuli, such as the irritating distractions of noises."

He looked me in the eye, "Doc, this is going to make a huge difference. I am going to use these ideas for sure. It's going to help me pitch with a deeper focus."

Opening night in Kansas City was a major civic event. Furthermore, the game against the Texas Rangers in early April was played in cold conditions. It was 39 degrees at game time, with a 9 mph wind. It was chilly and got much colder as the night went on. After playing four seasons in Kansas City Municipal Stadium, on April 10, 1973.

About 30 minutes prior to Paul's going to the bullpen to warm-up, I met him in the clubhouse. I had Paul sit down on a stool, look out about sixty feet and visualize his catcher, Jerry May, in a catcher's position with an umpire looking over his shoulder.

As I had Mark Littell in instructional league, I had Paul see and feel a series of high-quality pitches. I encouraged that he think of the pitches he wanted to pitch, feel his body go through the pitching motion and see a high-quality pitch busting through his target.

Paul replied, "This reminds me of something I saw on the news about astronauts at Cape Canaveral preparing for their various missions."

"It similar. They use simulators, but you use the bullpen mound and looking at your desired targets," thinking it was a good analogy for Paul to relate.

I then encouraged, "Paul remember to do this slow enough that you can decide on the pitch you want to pitch, feel the flow of energy through your body pitching that pitch, see the pitch produced by that great flow of energy and see it go through your target."

Paul said, "Am I trying to be a perfectionist by doing this? Am I going to set my expectations too high?"

I responded, "No, not it all. You are just waking up the parts of your brain that you are going to use in the game. You should also visual thinking for handling adversity, dealing with defensive plays, dealing with delays in the game or whatever could possibly happen. Cover everything that is possible but be realistic. You should prepare for everything that can happen so there are no surprises."

I then described the game situation as in the first three innings of the game and we went over each member of the Texas Rangers lineup. I had Paul feel and see the pitches going through Jerry May's glove in the desired pitching pattern. We went through each the entire lineup four times, the last time with the game on the line, runners in scoring position, and his pitching out of the stretch. It took about twenty minutes.

When we finished, I looked at him and let him talk.

"This is great. I am calm, focused, confident and I am ready to pound down," he walked over to the training room, but in the quiet clubhouse, I heard him say to himself, "I'm locked."

Paul pitched a nine-inning game against the Ted Williams managed Texas Rangers and won 12-1 giving up 5 hits, 3 walks, and 1 strikeout. Power hitter John Mayberry, the father of future major league player John Mayberry, Jr., led the Royals with a grand slam. The Royals inaugurated Royals Stadium with a win over the Texas Rangers.

Jack McKeon, "He pitched great. His pitch command was phenomenal. I sensed he was like a military sniper, picking his targets carefully and then busting them."

Paul continued to have a very good first 4 months and was 14-5 in early August, but then his arm started bothering him. He missed one start in his regular rotation. Upon returning to the rotation, he lost 5 games in a row.

He had lost 5 in a row when the team arrived in Oakland. In several of his recent games, he was pulled in the third or fourth inning after giving up a lot of hits His record had fallen to 15-11.

We met in the team's hotel lobby when the team arrived in Oakland. We chatted and he admitted, "Doc the last month with my arm bothering me, I just haven't been able to get focused like I was earlier in the season."

"Are you still doing your pre-game preparation as you did earlier?"

"No, not really," he paused. "It has sort of slipped my mind. I've spent most of my time in the trainer's room. I think guess I have just been worrying about my arm."

After further discussion and an emphasis on the greater need for resuming his pregame preparation approach he started earlier in the year, we agreed to meet in the clubhouse a half hour before he did his bullpen warmup.

I went to the clubhouse and found Paul sitting on a stool. He was staring off into space.

As I got closer he looked up and I said, "Paul, I want you to look out at the intended endpoint of your pitches and then see the intended pitch come backward about fifteen feet or so."

He did as I suggested. After seeing about ten or so pitches, he looked up at me and said, "I am getting the feel for those pitches. That is something I have lost recently, particularly on my breaking pitches."

I added, "You don't need to do this all the time. But it is a good idea to do in the bullpen until you gain the feel you are looking for. You can also do it with your last two to three warmup pitches between innings."

"So now, as you did earlier this year, look out sixty feet away, feel yourself pitching and see the result of quality pitches to your intended specific targets. Here's the A's line-up. Go through it at least three times," I instructed.

He proceeded to do it and on a cold, windy September night in Oakland Paul pitched 7 innings in a shutout of the Athletics 5-0 and brought the Royals within five games of first place of the reigning World Champions. It was the Royal's first time in a pennant race. They were in the hunt.

He went on to win his next five games and ended up the season with a 20-11 record and a 3.98 ERA. The Royals had a real ace, for the first time in their existence in their 4th season finished in second place.

Two years later, on June 24, 1975, Royals arrived in Anaheim and the team was not playing well. Jack McKeon told me to get together with Paul, that for some reason he had not pitched well all year.

Paul was 1-5 and only used in long relief. As I passed through the clubhouse, I observed Paul over by his locker sitting quietly.

After exchanging pleasantries, I asked, "Paul, are you doing the same things you did over the last couple of years."

"No, Doc," he said rather sharply.

Upon my asking him why not, he said, "Doc, I don't even want to talk about or think about pitching." Though it was obvious, he wanted to talk.

He went on "Every time I do all I can see is hanging pitches that are doubled off the wall. I don't even think about pitching. I just sit in the bullpen and try to not pay much attention to the game. If I get the call from Jack McKeon, I will just go through the motions."

Mystified, I didn't say anything and then asked, "What are you centering upon when pitch?"

"Everything. My mind is all over the place."

I was perplexed. Paul Splittorff was a top pitcher, one of the best in the American League. He was a very sharp guy. Very calm, very even type personality. Obviously, he was very frustrated.

I honored his desire not to talk much about pitching and we shifted to discussing things about our kids. He was very proud of his daughter Jennifer and his son Jamie. And I had my son Ryan with me.

I thought it over and decided there had to be a way to turn the tide. The next day, I prepared an audio tape that guided Paul through the pre-game preparation process that he formerly used effectively. I had no idea if he would use it

The next afternoon in the visitors' clubhouse, I spoke to Paul and said, "I want you to try something for me. When you throw in the bullpen, with your eyes, I want you to draw a line on the ground to your intended target. You just need to do it for about ten to fifteen feet. So look out on the ground, you will see your catcher in your peripheral vision, find a spot and just trace a line to your target."

He looked at me with a rather curious look.

"That will keep you in a fine center, out of your body and unaware of your surroundings. From there get your sign, take the time to feel and picture your pitch and let it go."

I could see he was doing it as he looked across the clubhouse floor. He then looked up, "I think this may help."

I then said, "One other thing, if you sense you aren't focused, if you sense a negative thought, quickly look at your catcher's left knee guard and quickly make three cycles to his right knee guard, back to the left and so on. When you finish, look right at the catcher's sign and start your routine."

He thought some more. I could tell he wasn't sure this would work for him.

I pointed out a shoe sitting in a cubicle across the clubhouse. "Paul, I am going to have you look at that shoe, but before you do it, look at the left side of that cubicle, then the right, do it three times and then look directly at the shoe."

He proceeded to do it and then looked at me with a wry smile, "You are right. The shoe looked clearer and closer to me. And, I wasn't thinking of anything but that shoe. When I pitched well in the past, the glove always looked close to me. This year it has looked 100 to 120 feet away. This can help."

"Paul, I assure you that will keep you from thinking. It will stop negative thoughts and it will allow you do follow your normal effective routine."

I then said, "Paul, since you are not in the rotation and don't know when you are going to pitch, here's something you can do. Every day at home or in your hotel room use this audio to help you feel and visualize throwing quality pitches. At first, ignore who the hitter is and who you are pitching against, but just feel and see a series of quality pitches to one of your catchers."

He nodded as if he was willing to do it.

"After a while go through the lineup of the team the Royals are opposing that day. See yourself performing successfully in all kinds of challenging situations. Do it daily for a week or so and see what happens. The worst is you will have wasted a little time."

He said, "Yeah, I will do it. I can't get any worse."

As the Royals left Anaheim, I was hoping that I had helped Paul get back on track A few days later, on June 29 he pitched effectively for 6.2 innings against the Chicago White

Sox. He lost 3-1 but only gave up 2 earned runs.

A month later, July 25, 1975, manager Jack McKeon was fired by the Royals and replaced by Whitey Herzog.

On July 29, Paul proceeded to pitch 7 innings against Minnesota and won 5-2 giving him his second win of the season. From there, he became a fixture once again in the Kansas City rotation. He pitched a 5-0 shutout against the Oakland A's on August 3. He won 4 games in a row prior to a loss and finished 9-10 where at one time he was 1-6. He went 8-4 over the last 12 outings of the season.

He then won 5 games in a row and ended up 8-4 the last 12 games of the season. 8-4 was quite a change from the 1-5 he was on June 24.

I never knew how much he used the audio tape, but his road trip roommate catcher Buck Martinez told me years later that he recalled hearing the audio almost daily when the team was on the road.

Martinez, subsequently managed the Toronto Blue Jays and became a popular national media personality, said, "I was Paul's roommate. I saw him doing his focusing drills, listening to the audio regularly. He would even do it on the bus to the ballpark. He definitely started pitching much better."

Buck went on, "When I gave him a sign, as he nodded in agreement, there was always a half second or so prior to his starting his motion. As a contrast, many pitchers are anxious and as soon as they see the sign they begin their motion. I could see that Paul was taking a moment for a quick thought, I sensed it as a moment of commitment before he began each pitch, and likely he was seeing the pitch before he got started."

In 1976, Paul was pitching well, had won 8 games in a row when he broke his finger in July. His record was 11-7 at the time, but he couldn't pitch for weeks.

In early September, we met when the Royals visited Anaheim. His finger had just been removed from a cast and he was frustrated and rather downcast.

He said, "I'm about recovered. I am afraid Whitey is not going to let me pitch until we either clinch or lose the Divisional Championship." And then he paused, "And the way it is going that may not be determined until the last game or two of the seasons."

He went on, "If we do win the Division we are going to be in the playoffs against the Yankees who are running away with the Eastern Division."

He then added, "I have been effective against the Yankees in the past, I expect Whitey is going to call upon me to pitch." He then added adamantly, "There is no way I can be ready to pitch."

I thought about his situation and suggested, "Paul, it is true that you aren't going to be able to physically get into pitching shape, but you can mentally."

"How's that?" he asked with a level of anxiousness.

"Well, every day, against the lineup the Royals are facing, you need to see and feel yourself throwing a series of pitches to each hitter. Just like you did when you prepared for a game you need to go through the line up three to four times. The first time you don't want to show your best pitches. The second time around have a man in scoring position. The third time around the game is getting more intense, and there are runners in scoring position. And then the fourth time around you are in the eighth or ninth inning, and you are preserving a win."

I paused, "Can you do that every day?"

He paused, "Well, yeah, I guess I can. It certainly won't hurt."

He shook his head sideways a bit and offered, "I should have thought of that."

"Paul, if you do that you will be mentally ready come playoff time and will give yourself the best chance to pitch well," I suggested.

"Makes sense. I'll do it," he confirmed.

Paul was right. He pitched one inning in September. And on Oct 3, after the Royals had clinched a playoff spot he got to pitch four innings in a losing cause.

But he was ready for the playoffs. He was the first Royals pitcher to win a postseason game, getting the decision in relief in Game 2 of the American League Championship Series against the Yankees. In 1976, he pitched in 2 games against the Yankees. He won 1 game in the series and had a 1.93 era. He did it while pitching only four innings in 3 months.

Unlike many great pitchers, Paul didn't have electric stuff, with neither an overpowering fastball nor a plunging slider. He relied instead on good command of several different pitches to keep hitters off stride.

A durable presence in the middle of the Royals' rotation, he started nearly 400 games, pitched more than 2,500 innings. His delivery, featuring a high leg kick, made him especially effective against left-handed hitters. He was known as well for his preparation, entering each game with an aggressive plan for how to pitch to each hitter. He became a mainstay of the Royals' staff during the 1970s as the club evolved from a weak expansion team into a powerful annual pennant contender.

Paul taught me that one's brain is more powerful than I ever imagined. From his positive experience with various ideas we discussed, I have been able to help many pitchers ever since.

Paul, after learning how to use a visual approach to pregame preparation, went from a .500 pitcher to a great career with the Kansas City Royals. Paul had a great career.

He won 166 games and lost 143, and his lifetime earned run average was 3.81. He was inducted into the Royals Hall of Fame in 1987, an honor well deserved.

Sadly, on May 25, 2011, Paul died of cancer in his Blue Springs, Missouri, home at the age of 64. The world lost an exceptional man on that day, and those that were fortunate to know him will miss him forever.

Perhaps Ewing Kauffman, Mark Littell, and Syd Thrift were a big part of Paul's success. For certain, Paul became a genius at "Picturing and feeling doing it, focusing, and then pitching the ball through his intended target."

As great as Paul was, from time to time I have thought, "Would he been as great if he hadn't learned what we initially developed at the Kansas City Royals Baseball Academy and the concepts that were initiated with his teammate Mark Littell?"

We'll never know for sure.

Chapter 4

STEVE BLASS
World Series MVP Then Totally Lost Pitch Command

In the early 1970, current Pittsburgh Pirates announcer, Steve Blass was famous for being the 1971 World Series MVP. In 1971, he had a 19 and 8 won-lost record and was 2nd in the Cy Young Award voting. As he entered the 1972 season, event greater success was expected. In 1972, Steve had an ERA of 2.48 while walking only 84 batters in 250 innings. He was a true ace of the Pirates pitching staff. Steve was within the top ten of all pitchers--the top ten of approximately 300 pitchers that pitched in Major League Baseball in 1972. Suddenly in 1973, at age 32, he lost his pitch command. It appeared to be a mechanical problem. He tried every mechanical and psychological approach available, but nothing worked. Until the end of the 1974 season, he could not pitch with a hitter standing in the batter's box. He learned from some balance drills how his balance was improved simply by focusing his full visual attention on a specific target. After the two years of misery, Steve found his lost pitch command one day prior to the end of the season, by getting visually focused on a specific target. He overcame the distractions, including the hitter's presence that had troubled him for two years. Though he found an apparent effective path to improving his command, by developing his visual focus, two years of struggle resulted in his retirement after the 1974 season.

When I worked with the Kansas City Royals, it was a result of the improved production of position player Ed Kirkpatrick. He went from a .224-lifetime hitter to a very productive hitter who hit over .300 most of the 1972 season,

On December 4, 1973, the Royals traded Ed Kirkpatrick along with Winston Cole, a Royals Baseball Academy graduate, and Kurt Bevacqua to the Pittsburgh Pirates for Nelson Briles and Fernando Gonzalez. It turned out to be a significant trade for the Royals as Briles was a proven starting pitcher. He became a starting pitcher and helped lead the Royals to the American League Divisional playoffs in 1976.

I was shocked to learn that Ed was no longer a Royal. He had been very productive and versatile player for the Royals. He was enjoyable to watch play. And he was becoming a very good hitter. After a hand injury, his batting average dropped from .300 to .275 but he kept battling.

After his trade to the Pirates, in spring training 1974, Ed called me in spring training and said, "Can you come to Bradenton. I need a refresher, and I would like for you meet with a couple of guys?"

Going to see the Pittsburgh Pirates and meet some of them was a thrill. Known as the Pittsburgh Lumber Company, these guys could hit. Batting practice sounded like a series of explosions on a military base.

Ed introduced me around the Pirate clubhouse to Manny Sanguillen, Richie Zisk, Doc Ellis, Bruce Kison, Willie Stargell, Jerry Ruess and many other guys. These guys were cool guys and very normal despite all of their success. This was one of the great teams of that era, perhaps the best.

Steve Blass, famous for his great 1971 World Series pitching resulting in his getting the MVP, reached out his hand and gave me a strong handshake. I thought, "This guy is a lot different than the one I have read about." He was as warm and friendly a fellow one could ever meet. I was very aware that he had such a difficult 1973 season.

A right-handed pitcher, Blass made his professional

debut with Kingsport in 1960 and his Major League debut with the Bucs on May 10, 1964. He joined the big league team permanently in 1966 and went on to pitch a total of 10 seasons in the Majors, compiling a 103-76 record, 57 complete games, and 16 shutouts in 282 games.

During a five-year span from 1968 thru 1972, Blass was one of the best pitchers in the National League as he compiled a 78-44 record, 50 complete games, and a 3.05 ERA. He won a career-high 19 games in 1972 and was named to the National League All-Star team that season.

In his third full season in the Majors in 1968, Steve went 18-6, leading the league with a .750 winning percentage while posting a 2.12 ERA, 12 complete games, and a career-high seven shutouts. His 2.12 ERA ranked fifth in the N.L.

He remains among the few starting pitchers to throw a complete game in Game Seven of a World Series.

For eight years Steve h ad been very successful. During the 1971 World Series, he pitched two complete nine-inning games, including the Championship game. He won both games as he recorded two complete-game victories, allowing only seven hits and two runs in 18 innings of work. He won the World Series MVP award.

In 1972, he had a 19 and 8 won-lost record and was 2nd in the Cy Young Award voting. That season Steve had an ERA of 2.48 while walking only 84 batters in 250 innings. He was a true ace of the Pirates pitching staff. Steve was within the top ten of all pitchers in Major League Baseball. That's the top ten of approximately 300 pitchers that pitched in Major League Baseball in1972.

Suddenly in 1973, he lost his pitch command. He couldn't throw strikes. He hit batters and walked many.

In 1973, he won only three games. He lost nine. He walked 84 batters in 89 innings and posted one of the highest ERAs among major league pitchers — 9.81. By July, at 32 years of age, he seldom pitched. He won only three games. He lost nine. He walked 84 batters in 89 innings and posted one of the highest ERAs among major league pitchers—9.81. By July, at 32 years of age, he seldom pitched. Articles about his demise were all over the baseball media.

He had reached levels of success as a Major League pitcher that very few pitchers had ever achieved. He was headed for a Hall of Fame career. He reached the pinnacle, was King of the Hill for a while, but, unfortunately, learned how difficult it was to stay there.

Ed said as he introduced me to Steve, "I told Steve how you have helped Paul Splittorff, Steve Busby, Mark Littell Dennis Leonard and other Royals pitchers and he wants to find out if he can do the same for him."

Steve said rather laughingly, "Doc, you've got your work cut out if you are going to help me," he paused and then added, "I'm a mess. When I am on the mound, I just can't concentrate. My mind goes a mile a minute, and I think of just about everything."

Ed said, "I told Steve you were the guy that could possibly help him."

"Doc, here's how bad I was last year. If I were the manager I wouldn't have used me," Blass said. "I was totally ineffective and wild. I started the season poorly but thought nothing of it. I had had poor starts before. I was 2-8 one year and turned it around. I had always been able to turn them around."

His jovialness disappeared as he described what had been going on, "But instead of snapping out of it, I got progressively worse. It probably was a mechanical thing at first. My motion was uncoordinated. I was hurrying my pitches. I had no rhythm. My body was moving faster toward the plate than my arm, and to compensate, my arm began rushing to catch up. The result was I was throwing pitches high and outside to right-handed batters and behind the heads of lefthanders."

Once hoping to rebuild Blass' confidence, manager Danny Murtaugh announced that he would start him in a game. Blass was terrified. "It was in Chicago," he says. "Six weeks before, the last time I pitched, I walked five batters in 1 innings. I roamed the streets of Chicago until 5:30 in the morning."

On the day before he is to pitch his second batting practice of the 1974 spring training, Steve said, "I never struggled at pitching before. I mean, I was never uncertain about whether or not I wanted to walk out to the mound. Now, it scares me. Frankly, it scares the hell out of me. You have no idea how frustrating it is. You don't know where you're going to throw the ball. You're afraid you might hurt someone. You know you're embarrassing yourself, but you can't do anything about it. You're helpless. Totally afraid and helpless."

Steve was an archetypical Woody Allen as he was forever joking about himself and his pitching.

On our initial meeting, I did not ask Steve any questions about what had occurred in the last couple of years. My questions were about his approach to throwing a quality pitch in the World Series and the following year.

"Back in 1972 when you pitched your best pitches, what were you thinking about?" I probed.

Steve thought a few moments and said, "It was just all so easy. I didn't have to think about my pitching motion. I just let it happen."

"Were you thinking about anything? I asked.

"I think my thoughts then were about what pitch I needed to make to get the guy out."

He then added, "Yeah, I was thinking about the hitter and not thinking about myself?"

I asked, "Can you remember seeing the pitch before you threw it?"

He paused and responded, "Yeah, I think so. I would sense a pitch I wanted to throw, and I would see the hitter swinging and missing, or swinging and popping the pitch up or hitting three hop ground ball."

"Were you aware of your body's actions?" I probed further.

"No, not at all. I guess my mechanics were okay, but I had no idea. I just pitched the ball to where I wanted it to go."

"So you had a target you were throwing that pitch to?" I asked.

"Yeah, I think so. But the target wasn't Manny's glove," he thought further. "It actually was pitching to a zone."

"Was it like a window?" I asked trying to get him to be more specific in his memory.

"Yes, that's it. After deciding what the hitter couldn't hit, I would focus on a small window over home plate I wanted the ball to go through."

After discussing what he thought his problem was in 1973, it became apparent that he was not focused on the pitch he was going to throw but was focused on the possible bad effect the pitch might cause. In fact, he had a very broad focus, a soft center and had given up on focusing on any target

In the short time we had available, I probably didn't go into in enough depth and certainly did not put him through any of my drills that would have helped him to understand it better. I did give him an understanding about centering. We review soft and fine centering as well as internal and external centering.

We discussed focusing one pitch at a time by preparing for the pitch with a good picture of the pitch and then focusing on the target. I recall saying, "For now, let's just work on getting a small target before you start your pitching action."

He said, "Good idea. I will aim small and hopefully miss small." Steve was very glib. I wanted to believe that he could take the information and put it to work.

Steve impressed me as a very bright guy. In retrospect, I am sure part of his issue was he was too smart. He was very agreeable. I didn't realize that being agreeable didn't mean he would actually understand what I was talking about and subsequently put it to use.

It wasn't the case. He had another miserable season. He was 2-8 in AAA with a 9.74 era. He was wild and hit a lot of guys. No doubt, he needed a lot more hands-on training, and change was not going to be easy.

In August 1974, I got a call from Pittsburgh Pirate General Manager Joe Brown.

He said, "Steve Blass is still having a lot of difficulties. He has said of all the people he has listened too, and ideas he has tried, your approach makes the most sense."

Mr. Brown went on, "We are playing San Francisco next week. I would like to send Steve Blass out a few days early to see you."

With the Pirates playing the Giants in a 3 game weekend series Steve came to Davis, California and spent a couple of days Wednesday and Thursday.

I did a complete evaluation of his concentration skills and his overall coordination. Most glaring, I found that Steve had very poor balance. As soon as he tried to do something while standing on one leg, which is what occurs in pitching, his lower body tightened up and his overall coordination deteriorated. It was very observable as we had him do drills on a walking rail, a balance platform, and a mini-trampoline.

We discussed something he had mentioned to me earlier

in spring training. He had said that he really struggled to pitch in the wind. I pointed out to him that what occurs in the wind is we tend to tighten up our muscles to brace against it. In fact, we tend to lose our flexibility and our coordination deteriorated.

"That makes total sense to me," he responded. "The wind really bothers me."

I felt we were on to something. Though not old at age 32, I could sense that when he was in his early twenties, his balance was probably better. And, just a small loss, for whatever reason might have been enough to make it impossible for him to find his consistent pitching delivery.

In those years, there was not much medical knowledge on dizziness, vertigo, and related conditions. Perhaps today a problem could have been diagnosed. Also, today the strength and conditioning programs often involve balance and likely in these days he would have better developed his balance.

One thing for certain, when one has an issue with their balance; it is very difficult to focus visually on a target.

Focusing on a fixed target can be difficult enough, but focusing on a small window of air, suspended in space, was really difficult. So I concluded that his lack of good balance triggered his difficulty to focus visually on his desired window. From there his coordination suffered, and he was unable to execute a pitching motion consistently, most of which was on one leg.

He appeared to be having a lot of fun. But he just couldn't handle the basic coordination that was needed to do much on the trampoline.

I had Steve go through his pitching motion with his eyes closed. It was shockingly inadequate. I grabbed him each time to keep him from falling down. I had seen something with several other athletes I had done this with but none struggled with it like Steve. Furthermore, many athletes, kickers, golfers, hitters and others, could do this flawlessly after I encouraged that they focus properly on a small target even with their eyes closed. Often they did it almost as well as if their eyes were open. Invariably these athletes were quite proficient in their physical actions

"Doc, I'm going to hurt myself," he laughed but had a more serious look on his face.

We spent a couple of days doing various drills and discussing various pitching issues. I learned that though Steve bought into my recommendations in spring training when he started his pitching motion his attention always went to his body. The effect of this was though he started his pitching motion while focused on his target, when he began to throw his primary awareness went to his body, and visual focus became very broad. Furthermore, at times his focus would go directly to the hitter. Steve was a compassionate guy and did not want to hit hitters and often was thinking about what he thought the hitter must have feared about getting hit.

From my perspective, Steve's issues had a lot to do with his faulty equilibrium. I viewed pitching as an amazingly complex coordination act, the majority of which took place on one leg. Not only did he push off on one leg, but he landed on one foot and as the ball was released the other foot and leg were still in the air.

I knew that poor body balance resulted in a stiff body, no matter how strong. And when the body was stiff there was very little rhythm and ability to coordinate the body parts.

I explained, "Steve, even if you have prepared properly for pitching a great pitch, even if you are focused properly, even if you have great confidence in your pitch, when you get into your delivery your subconscious brain senses you are struggling with your balance and it triggers your body to tighten up. It's a natural reflex. When that occurs, you are going to lose control of the fine muscles in your arms, and, more importantly, fingers. When this occurs, you can't have pitch command because your fingers don't have the kind of loose grip you need for the ball to come out of your hand properly."

"Doc, I think you have nailed it. In spring training, I think I was doing all the right things, prepared for the pitch and focused pretty good prior to the pitch, but once I got near the release of the ball I lost focus and no sense of what the ball feels like. I just didn't know it was my lack of good balance was screwing everything up."

My belief at the time was the most important tie for a tight focus was when the ball left the fingertips. I also believed that that was the critical moment that the body needed to amazingly relaxed and stable so that the wrist, hand, and fingers would be maximally relaxed and loose.

Even with repetitive efforts in many of the drills, Steve was slow to improve. My interpretation was that his body awareness, the control of his energy expenditure was not very effective. He also didn't what I liked to refer to as visual trust.

Visual trust began to evolve when I decided to go back to each drill and have him visually fine center on a small, meaningful target and then step into the drills. My plan was that as soon as could see a slight wavering of his balance I would put my hands on him and stabilize him so that he wouldn't fail. Though it took time, he began to find that if he stayed locked on to his visual target, his body would relax and he was able to maintain his balance for slightly longer periods.

He responded, "I am very surprised how much more stable I feel if I lock on to a visual target."

"Steve, this is one of the reasons that when you pitch, in the bullpen or in a game, you need to fine center on a portion of your catcher's glove—the webbing, the crevice, a knot in the leather string."

"Doc, I get it. I think I need to spend my offseason doing balance drills and when I do them, I will make sure that I am visually locked in. I think I can get better at it."

And then he added, "You are so right about visual trust. And, I don't think I have had it."

I could see that this had become a real teaching moment. I think he was gaining some satisfaction that his pitching struggles were not just due to his lack of effort, but possibly due to a real physical issue that was affecting his ability to focus.

I commented, "Steve, athleticism at a high level, like pitching is not simple. It isn't just physical, it isn't just mental, and it just isn't visual. It's a somewhat delicate integration of everything working together. I like to call integration."

Steve then revealed, "I've never been very coordinated. In fact, even when I had successful seasons pitching it usually took about 3 months of pitching regularly before I would get consistent. I wasn't concerned until June when it became apparent I wasn't getting to the point I ordinarily was."

My thoughts were that with 3 months of pitching regularly each year, Steve developed a better balance capability. Perhaps subconsciously he got a little more visual and to pitch effectively. But each offseason and each year of getting older, it finally caught up with him.

I was confident he was beginning to get it. But one problem I could see is that he needed to pitch to hitters. This was an issue because the Pirates were not going to use him the rest of the season.

So that he could pitch, something he had not done for a few weeks, I got permission to use the UC Davis soccer field. I was able to get a local young man, Brandt Cooper, who had played local high school baseball to be Steve's catcher.

We did on flat ground on in open space, without a backstop.

I told Steve to take the time to see his pitch in advance, then get visually riveted on the webbing in the catcher's glove and maintain that focus until the pitch hit the glove.

Steve put into play my recommendations and threw 30-40 pitches very effectively.

He stopped for a moment and said, "Doc, this is rather amazing. I don't think I have had one thought about my body. It sort of seems automatic."

He had command of most pitches unless he attempted to throw a pitch with 100% effort. I asked that he back down and throw each pitch with 80-90% effort and he responded with excellent pitches once again.

I was aware that because of his body equilibrium challenges when he went to 100% effort he lost his fine muscle control, rhythm and timing of his body part's various movements.

I gave him a routine to work in the coming offseason to enhance his balance and to learn how to control his energy flow as he executed his pitching.

He was outwardly pleased, and then said, "But I've thrown good bullpens. My problem is when a hitter is up there."

I quickly thought to myself, "How are we going to handle that?"

I then thought, "I know how to see the ball coming out of a pitcher's hand, and I know how to roll with the pitch, so, heck, I'll be the hitter."

I must admit I was challenging myself at that time. I hadn't faced a pitcher for almost ten years, and none we of the Steve Blass capability. After all, he was the World Series MVP."

I stepped in. Later, Steve told me that he was also scared. He was polite and didn't say it, but later said he thought, "Hey, this guy is out of shape. He's not a trained baseball hitter. This is going to be tough."

I once again encouraged that he make an effort to get visually locked on Brandt Cooper's glove. Of course, I did this in an effort for self-preservation. I knew I could roll away from the pitch but really didn't want to get hit.

I looked at Brandt and he looked back as if to say, "Are you sure you want to do this?" He didn't say it, so neither Brandit or I responded.

Steve proceeded to throw about twenty more pitches. He was pretty locked in. He threw about 60-70% strikes, and none of his balls were far away from the strike zone.

When we finished, Steve said, "Wow, I haven't thrown like that in over two years."

He went on, "I was really focused on the crease in Brandt's glove. I am amazed that I was not aware of your presence. The last couple of years I think I have been more aware of the opposing hitter than I have my catcher's glove."

"With this approach do you think you have found an effective way to get back to what you used to do?" I inquired.

"Darn rights, this is ought to work. It is by far the best I have pitched in two years," he responded with a nice smile of satisfaction on his face.

He then said, "It is rather amazing to think that for two years I have been grinding on my mechanics to solve my problems, and the solution is to use my eyes to intently focus on my target."

Steve left Davis Friday morning after we had breakfast and joined the Pirates for their three-game series in Candlestick. He asked me to join him in the clubhouse prior to the Friday night game. He took me around the clubhouse and introduced me to several other pitchers and had me talked to them about my approach. He told them he thought he had finally found what he needed to do to turn around his career. He introduced me to Doc Ellis and Jerry Ruess and they expressed being very interested and spoke to me at length.

That winter on an East Coast trip, I visited Steve in Pittsburgh in November and he was in great spirits. It was great to see him so relaxed. We reviewed what we had worked on, and he seemed to be set to reinvent his pitching career. We spent some time with his friend Dave Giusti, the Pirates great relief pitcher. He told Giusti that he thought he had finally figured things out, thanks to my ideas.

I called him just prior to spring training with the intent of setting sometimes to get together in Bradenton, Florida and he shocked me.

"Doc, I've decided to hang it up."

I am sure he could sense the shock that I was going through, and he then added, "I just don't want to go through all of the press and fanfare again. Even if I pitched better, I just concluded I didn't want to deal with it anymore."

I recall being speechless, but I fully understood. But I was so disappointed because I highly believed he had an approach that would help him regain his pitching skills. In fact, I thought he could end up being better than ever.

Steve broke the silence again and said, "I've had a great career in baseball, but I have a very good job offer with Jostens's, the company that makes team and high school graduation rings. I think it is the right thing to do."

He then added, "It's too bad you and I couldn't have gotten together three seasons ago before everything fell apart for me. I think if I would have previously learned about focus and trained my balance I would not have had such problems."

After I had thought further about Steve over the

following weeks, his decision began to make sense. He was a confident guy in life and knew that he would succeed at other opportunities. In fact, he had had so much success as a Major League pitcher that his career was complete. There really was no need to endure the stress of turning his career around. It was time to have fun and enjoy life. And Steve knew how to enjoy life fully and he had the great talent of making everyone around him enjoy life. He reinvented himself and after a short career at Jostens switched careers and became a beloved, longtime broadcaster for the Pirates.

So, just prior to becoming 33, a great pitcher of that era retired. Baseball lost a great guy, but it was understandable that he opted for some peace and calmness in his life. After ten seasons in Major League Baseball, he had accomplished a lot.

He last quality pitches were thrown out there in the outfield of the University of California at Davis baseball field. He pitched very effectively against an over the hill, a former college pitcher. Incidentally, I didn't have a bat in my hand.

My experience with Steve Blass further solidified my belief that consistent, high-level athletic performance required a firm foundation of skills and skill-sets. His lack of high-quality balance, rhythm and coordination were definitely a reason that he had difficulty in focusing. It was too bad that when he entered professional baseball at age seventeen that he couldn't have started a strength and conditioning pogrom that involved agility, pushed his balance capability. No doubt it would have aided and likely lengthened his career.

My experience also further confirmed my belief that pitchers needed to learn how to pitch to a specific visual target. Moving the focus from a specific physical target to a small window is just fine once there was some consistency in the pitching motion. If focusing on a window was not working, then reverting to a specific physical target was in order. Windows are fine. They just aren't easy to depend upon consistently. The idea of picturing the trajectory of the intended pitch through a window to a final, physical target is the best of methods.

I regret I couldn't have spent more time with Steve Blass in spring training, 1974. In effect, we had a great meeting, but it was one episode. I believe that if I could have seen him every couple of weeks for two to three months he would have improved and had a better 1974 season. His situation was just too complex for a single episode to be effective. But it wasn't because he was a headcase, it wasn't due to motivation, he simply had some resolvable physiological issues that adversely affected his ability to focus.

I learned a lot from working with Steve Blass. I regret that I can't really say that he learned a lot from me that benefited his career. If I had an opportunity again to work with Steve, I would have requested the opportunity to see him pitch in the bullpen, and on game day, I would want to watch his pregame preparation, his pregame bullpen, his actions on the bench. And, of course, would carefully have watched him take the mound and go about his business.

After the bullpen workouts and games, we would have reviewed what occurred just prior to various pitches and as the pitches were pitched. I am confident that with this level of interaction Steve's issues could have been minimized and he could have returned to his excellent pitching capability.

For certain, his career would have been prolonged if when he was successful in his earlier years if he would have developed a Personal Performance And Focus Plan. A good plan would have assured that he, on each pitch, "picturing doing it, feeling it, focusing and then pitch the ball through a specific target."

Chapter 5

OREL HERSHISER
59 Consecutive Scoreless Innings

Orel Hershiser developed his own effective approach including a focusing plan and used it on every pitch. His approach was very consistent. A minor league .500 pitcher, he learned from playing golf a focusing approach he became committed to that worked successfully. Orel went from 16-16 record in 1987 to 23-5 in 1988 and a record 59 consecutive scoreless innings. One of the greatest pitching performances over a period of time followed a small tweak in his approach. At one point, his physical talents were a large part of his success, but after a severe arm injury he had to rely more on his mental abilities. Having a good routine, an effective process prior to the arm injury helped him recover more effectively once he recovered. He went on to ten more seasons six of which he had a winning record. It was an amazing accomplishment. Specific steps he used in his personalized plan are described, steps that can be used by most every pitcher.

In January 1988, a friend of mine for the prior fifteen years Los Angeles Dodgers Hitting Coach Ben Hines asked if I could come to the Dodgers winter workout. Ben wanted to introduce me to some of the position players getting ready for spring training.

Ben knew that I had helped many players with their developing a consistent visual approach to their game and wanted to get me to work with the Dodgers. He was aware I had worked with the pitching staffs of the San Diego Padres

1984 World Series team, previously with the pitching staff of the Kansas City Royals and in the prior two seasons with the Pittsburgh Pirates.

Ben introduced me to Orel Hershiser, the young Los Angeles Dodger's star pitcher. At that time, the 29-year-old Orel Hershiser, as the Dodger's ace had just come off a 16-16 season with a 3.06 ERA. But in 1985 at age 26 he had an unbelievable record of 19-3 with a phenomenal 2.03 ERA.

Prior to throwing in the bullpen, Orel was cordial but he didn't want to talk very much. Wisely I think he was cautious to allow anyone disrupt his own ideas.

When I sensed the right moment I asked him a direct question "What is your most effective routine that you follow from pitch to pitch?"

His response surprised me a bit when he said, "Prior to 1970 I was a .500 pitcher in the minor leagues. From playing a lot of golf, I came across a couple of ideas that have helped me."

Upon asking what they were, he said, "Well, I don't discuss it with anyone. I just do it, and it works for me."

After throwing in the bullpen, he came over and was ready to talk a little more. He said, "My routine for each pitch begins with seeing the hitter's reaction to my previous pitch. At that time, I decide what my next pitch is going to be and where I plan to locate it."

"What was your focus on when you released the ball?" I asked.

"Scioscia's glove," he replied. Mike Scioscia was the Los Angeles Dodgers full-time catcher.

I further probed, "Do you visualize anything."

He thought, "Well, I don't know if you would call it visualizing, but one I decide upon the pitch, I picture how I am going to release that pitch. It's sort of a picture of my arm and wrist action and includes my exact release action."

Then he said, "In fact because it helps me in golf, I do that three times before I step on the rubber."

That really got my attention. Visualizing or picturing an action once takes a lot of concentration. To do it three times takes high-level concentration skills. Furthermore, it takes a lot of energy.

Orel went on to explain, "Once I step on the rubber I take a rather full breath and then exhale. I do that every time. Then, I look out at a specific spot about fifteen away from my catcher, Mike Scioscia. From that spot, just like I do when I putt in golf, I use my eyes to trace a line directly to my intended target in relationship to his body."

I then asked, "What's next?"

"Not much," he said. "Once I see the Mike's signs just look at the target, start my motion and let it go."

Later, I told Orel, "Your routine is terrific. It's a great plan. Is there anything about it you would like to have work better?

"No," he responded, "other than I commonly run out of gas after about 5 innings. In fact, after a game, I am totally mentally exhausted.

I thought about what he described and then decided to ask him, "Why do you picture your mechanics three times?"

He replied, "I don't know. I just did it that way when I was struggling a few years ago, and it seemed to work in golf as well as in pitching."

I said, "Your use of three pictures is of course very good, and without question the right thing to do if you are struggling with your release of your pitches. But it does take a lot of mental energy. If you are pitching well perhaps, you can save some mental energy if you picture the release once."

He thought about it and then replied, "I think you are right. That does make sense."

I went on, "Now if you do that, I have another suggestion. Once you get your sign from Mike, picture and feel the last fifteen feet of your intended pitch's trajectory going through your target."

He thought and then said, "That sounds interesting. I've never done that. I will give it a try. I like the idea of pitching through the target."

I would like to have more time with Orel, but felt I made the most of the opportunity. A few days later the Dodgers headed to Vero Beach for spring training

I didn't see Orel again. In watching him on television, I could see that after he had appeared to have gotten his sign from his catcher Mike Scioscia there was always a pause, perhaps a half second to a second, before he started his pitching motion. I expect that was the moment that Orel was visualizing the pitch he intended to throw.

In 1988, Hershiser arguably put together one of the best single seasons in pitching history. That year, he led the league with 23 wins and 15 complete games. He finished the season with a record 59 consecutive scoreless innings pitched, breaking the mark held by former Dodger great Don Drysdale of 58. Then he pitched 8 more scoreless innings in his next start, Game 1 of the NLCS, but the post-season innings do not count toward the record. He also won his first Gold Glove.

He was unanimously selected as the Cy Young Award winner, with a record of 23–8 and a 2.26 ERA.

Hershiser then capped his historic season in the World Series by pitching a shutout in Game 2 and allowing two runs in a complete game in the clinching victory in Game 5, winning the World Series MVP Award.

In the 1988 National League Championship Series between Hershiser's Dodgers and the New York Mets, Hershiser not only started Games 1 and 3 but recorded the final out in Game 4 in relief for a save. He then pitched a shutout in Game 7. He was selected MVP of the series.

Hershiser is the only player to receive the Cy Young Award, the Championship Series MVP Award, a Gold Glove, and the World Series MVP Award in the same season. He later was awarded both The Sporting News Pitcher of the Year and Sports Illustrated Magazine's Sportsman of the Year award for his accomplishments in 1988.

Orel went from 16-16 record in 1987 to 23-5 in 1988 and a record 59 consecutive scoreless innings. It was an incredible achievement.   Apparently he no longer got mentally exhausted as he pitched in the later innings of the 15 complete games he pitched.

I suspect the slight changes to his focus plan reduced his mental and physical exhaustion and pitching nine innings became easier.

Most importantly, Orel figured out himself how to have a consistent approach to each pitch he pitched in a game. He had a personal focus plan and a personalized approach. Playing golf at a high level gave him some of his answers. With his great plan, he didn't leave things to chance.

After arm surgery the next season he pitched another 12 seasons. But he was never quite as good as he was in 1988. Of course, very few Major League Pitchers have been that good. Likely his focus plan and approach helped Orel succeed despite some physical limitation.

His personal focus plan kept him focused on each pitch, one pitch at a time. It was specific, comprehensive, and repeatable as it kept him from focusing on different focal points inconsistently. He gave up hits, he gave up runs, but he stuck to his plan.

He had a great 18 season career. Prior to his arm injury, that plan had him on his way to Baseball's Hall of Fame.

Perhaps Ewing Kauffman, Mark Littell, Paul Splittorff and Syd Thrift were a part of Orel's success.

For certain he possessed his own personalize focusing plan.

As great as Orel was, from time to time I have thought, "Would he been as great if he hadn't learned what we initially developed at the Kansas City Royals Baseball Academy and the concepts that were initially proven by Mark Littell and Paul Splittorff?"

We'll never know for sure.

Chapter 6

GREG MADDUX
The Pitching Genius

You'll learn how this Hall of Fame pitcher, already a proven major league pitcher with the Chicago Cubs became a recognized pitching genius. By refining his focus, he lowered his earned run average significantly and increased his won-loss record in 1992 to win his first of four Cy Young Awards. You will learn how he took advantage of "what" opposing hitters could and could not see. When all the other pitchers were stressing over the pitching mechanics, over the radar gun readings of their fastball, and all kinds of other things, Greg wanted to know what hitters could see and what was difficult for them to see. You will learn how opposing hitters don't see slight changes of speed of the same pitch and master the ability to reduce their ability to square the balls solidly. You'll gain further insights on how to have a marksman-like focus, as your visual sense becomes dominant. This visual focus, just like it did for Maddux, will allow your subconscious mind to be free to assist you, a relaxed body and total concentration in the moment with a clear mind. When you also get into Maddux's state of high-performance focus, you will lose yourself in the action and be free of self-conscious thoughts and anxiety. It's also when you are free of awareness of your body and you win the test of your intention, your steadiness of focus, and the discipline in which you prepare for each pitch!

Greg Maddux is a great example of the fallacy of an old saying, "Nice guys finish last." Greg was and is as nice a guy as they come, and he was consistently a very effective pitcher. In fact, he was one of the most consistent pitchers of modern times. He earned a reputation as being a pitching genius as he exhibited the epitome of pitching brilliance.

In his 23-year career, Maddux was considered a shoe-in for his first eligible year to the Baseball Hall of Fame in 2014. In fact, Maddux's 97.2% of the vote was the highest percentage for any player since 2007, when Cal Ripken and the late great Tony Gwynn were elected on 98.5% and 97.6% of the ballot respectively.

Nicknamed "The Professor" for his amazing ability to make good pitches, Maddux was the first pitcher to win 4 consecutive Cy Young awards (1992-1995). He won 355 games, good for 8th on the all-time list. None of the other 7 pitchers pitched a game after 1965. In association with his winning ways, he also currently holds the record for the most consecutive seasons with 15+ wins, an incredible 17 seasons.

In my experiences with Greg, I will always remember him as just a regular guy. That included prior to his first Cy Young winning season, during the next three and winning four Cy Young awards. He never changed.

He was smart. He was very receptive to good ideas and very effective at weeding out the ones that were not he didn't think were relevant to him.

Maddux relied on his command, composure, and guile to outwit hitters. Though his fastball touched 93 mph in his first few seasons, pitch velocity was not his hallmark. He was noted for the late movement on his sinker, which, combined with his peerless control, made him known as an excellent groundball pitcher. While his strikeout totals were average, hitters were often unable to make solid contact with his pitches.

Greg grew up in Las Vegas and was like the famous magicians and illusionists. Like a master illusionist, he produced pitches that appeared like an optical illusion as they left opposing hitters swinging through balls, hitting them weakly and making outs.

It was a beautiful sight to watch Greg pitch. To the general observer, he wasn't that impressive. He wasn't as big as most pitchers, his delivery was not herky jerky. His pitches didn't look overwhelming. Simply, opposing hitters couldn't hit him very effectively.

My work with Greg started when Syd Thrift invited me to work with the Chicago Cubs in 1992. Syd was hired as the Assistant General Manager by the new General Manager Larry Himes. Syd's primary responsibility was to bring in new player development ideas to the Cubs and because we had worked together for twenty years at that time, he was convinced what I had to offer would be beneficial to the Cubs.

The prior year, Syd, wanting to stay in baseball part-time joined me in working with several organizations. He persuaded his friends Los Angeles Dodgers General Manager Fred Claire, New York Mets General Manager Frank Cashen, and San Francisco Giants General Manager Al Rosen on utilizing our combined services to training their managers, coaches, and some of their players on the visual side of the game.

With the Cubs initially only a few of the pitchers were open to our ideas. The manager, Jim Lefebvre and his pitching coach, Billy Connors, did not appear to be on board with us. They didn't know that what we were doing was attempting to help them win as a manager and coach. But they didn't take the time to find out.

Veteran pitchers Mike Morgan, Greg Maddux, Bob Scanlan and Chuck McElroy, were very interested. Jeff Robinson, as a former Pirate, already was familiar with our approach from our work in the Pirates organization. Jeff was always open to our uncommon pitching ideas.

The initial meeting with Greg Maddux in early spring training 1992 was remarkable. He had earned the position of number one pitcher on the Cubs staff. In his prior four years, he was 67-46 with an era of 3.25. That was a very impressive with the Chicago Cubs where being a successful starting pitcher was very difficult, particularly on windy days in Wrigley Field.

Upon first meeting, I expected to meet another young baseball star with a big ego. That was not the case at all. Greg was a very pleasant young man. In fact, it was refreshing to meet a successful young pitcher who was so open and willing to talk.

It was enjoyable working with Greg because he was open and receptive to discussing pitching and the consideration of varying viewpoints.

Greg typically merely listened and then synthesized what he thought was relevant to him and put it into action. He always asked great questions, some of which we did not have the answer. Much of what we encouraged the pitching staff to do, he was already doing. The same was true with his friend from his hometown, Mike Morgan. Mike was a veteran of 11 seasons at that time.

Morgan was mature. Greg was also despite being only 26 years old. His maturity and thought processes were very advanced for his age.

We explained to Greg how a fine focus on a small area in the catcher's glove was desired at the point of pitch release. We explained the balance, fine muscle control and visual centering ideas. We also covered various benefits of pitcher's seeing the pathway of their pitch to their intended target before starting their pitching motion.

Most of what we discussed he was already doing, but he appeared to appreciate the confirmation that he was doing all the right things.

During the 1992 season, Syd and I watched Greg's pitching performances very carefully. In a sense, we scouted his focus, expecting to see a breakdown. However, what we saw was a guy who could focus on every pitch as if it was the only pitch he would ever throw. He did get mad at times, but it turned out he didn't get mad at an umpire's call or a hitter squaring his pitch.

What Greg got mad, and it would occur from time to time, it was about was the realization is upset that he didn't make a good decision prior to the pitch. He wasn't as mad about the result, it was just that he thought he should have known better.

Upon occasion, a hitter would tee off on him, and if it was a hit off of the proper pitch, he simply tipped his hat. If it was a bad decision on his part or a loss of pitch command, he would throw a fit until he stepped back up on the mound to face the next hitter. Invariably, he refocused on the first pitch to the next hitter. He was unique and extraordinary.

1992 Greg went 20-11 with an era of 2.18 Greg was the first pitcher in major league history to win the Cy Young Award for four consecutive years, 1992 through 1995 seasons. He was clearly the best pitcher in the National League. In fact, Greg's already successful career took an upward path and after 1992, he had 13 consecutive winning seasons 230 – 110. During those four consecutive seasons, he had a 75–29 record with an incredible 1.98 earned run average.

Surprisingly the Cubs decided not to sign Greg when he was a free agent. Twenty years later the Cubs have not recovered. Ironically, in early 1993 he signed with the Atlanta Braves another team I was working with at the time.

Greg looked up to the new but veteran Cubs pitcher Mike Morgan. Among other things, Mike was a hunter. He spent much of offseason in the mountains.

One day in the clubhouse I was with Syd Thrift and we started chatting with Mike. Syd talked about he liked to go bird hunting.

"I have found shooting a gun has helped me a lot pitching," Mike remarked.

Wanting to keep the discussion going forward I said, "A marksman-like focus will allow you to lose awareness of your body and the related discomforts and frustrations the body produces. With a marksman-like focus, you will perform at a higher level because your natural skills and talents function at your best when you are on automatic pilot.

Syd then said, "Consider the type of focus required if you were a sniper bunkered in a hillside in the mid-east."

Morgan asked, "What kind of focus does a sniper have?"

I answered, "A marksman-like focus is a more intense focus, is held longer and one in which we sense we are more riveted to sensing a specific feeling, a specific sound, a specific thought or a specific visual target. A marksman-like focus will allow you to lose awareness of your body and its related discomforts and frustrations. With a marksman-like focus, you will perform at a higher level because your natural skills and talents function at your best when you are on automatic pilot."

Syd said, "We already know that a critical component in reaching our goals is focus. The problem is that focusing is not too easy with all the temptations and distractions that surround us."

I added, "Good snipers pull the trigger once they're calm. Simply put, when you are calm, relaxed, you get things done effectively. Stress is a state in which your body is in alarm, and you're fighting to keep control. When you operate under stress, you may think you are getting a lot of things done, but you may be wasting your ammunition. You are simply not accurate and will ultimately stress those around you. You've liked heard or read from most pitchers when they were at the top of your game, say they were thinking of nothing and time seems to slow down. That occurred when they were in a marksman-like state of focus."

Morgan looked over at Maddux and said, "That describes the kind of focus I have when I am pitching well."

Greg said, "Same with me."

By this time, some of the younger Cubs pitchers were nearby and I could see their expressions of admiration. Among them were Jose Bautista, Bob Scanlan, and Turk Wendell.

I commented, "It is very powerful as a marksman-like focus provides you an unobstructed pathway to the immense powers and physical abilities that lie within your subconscious mind."

Syd added, "You may have had a marksman-like focus when you were one hundred percent prepared and focused on winning an important game. It may have occurred when you were so sick or tired that you couldn't think of anything or it may have happened when you were very relaxed."

Morgan said, "When I am hunting deer and am on the top of my game, the target I am shooting at looks closer, clearer and bigger. The same is true when I pitch as the target looks larger, clearer and closer."

Greg nodded in agreement.

I added, "When you have a marksman-like focus, your visual sense was dominant. This visual focus allowed your subconscious mind to be free to assist you, a relaxed body and total concentration in the moment with a clear mind."

Syd added, "When you get into this state of mind, you lose yourself in the action and are free of self-conscious thoughts and anxiety. It's also when you are free of awareness of body parts, distractions, and stress. It is very unique because time seems to slow down. Fun and enjoyment of competing are at a peak — pure and unspoiled."

At another time, late in spring training in 1992, the professor-like looking pitcher looked at me and asked me point blank, "I want to understand better what hitters can see?"

Now this was something. When all the other pitchers were stressing over the pitching mechanics, over the radar gun readings of their fastball, and all kinds of other things he wanted to know what hitters could see and what was difficult for them to see. That question started quite a dialog that continued for several years.

I explained to Greg that hitters could occasionally see a lot more than they do, but typically a hitter's focus is on what they are feeling within their body or they were focused on thoughts. In effect, despite good eyes, they didn't see very well.

"When they are focused within their body or on thoughts, they are in a general focus and they don't see the seams rotation. Every pitch looks to them as coming at the same speed, the pitcher's typical fastball speed."

I went further "In fact, most hitters see and react to a pitcher's arm flying through the release area. They see a fast arm and they start their actions."

I told him, "Most hitters don't see slight changes of speed very well at all. It's as if they are blind to small changes of speed. Invariably that disrupted their timing and they wouldn't square the ball very well."

I clarified, "If it is a big change of speed they see a trajectory change, but if it is a slight change of speed they don't register it and, as a result, they can have a great swing bad timing."

I recall his responding, "As I think about it, I can remember seeing that happen. I thought it was the type of pitch, but you are saying it was the slight change of speed that got them. I think you are right," he responded.

I explained, "Greg most of the hitters in the major leagues see every pitch as coming at the same speed. As I have said, they don't see slight changes. As a result, they are primed for the fastball speed most of the time."

He asked a good question, "Is it a form of blindness?"

"No, not true blindness," I responded. "It is a bit like color blindness or color deficiency. Not many people are actually color blind, in that their world looks white, black and gray. But many people, particularly men have a color deficiency. Color deficient people don't see color unless it is highly apparent."

I paused and then went on, "90-95% of major league hitters are velocity deficient, which is a nice way of saying blind to seeing velocity, and they don't see a slight change of velocity unless it is highly apparent."

"Really," he inquired, "Who are the ones' that aren't?"

"From testing their ability I can tell you Barry Bonds, Tony Gwynn, John Kruk, Kevin McReynolds, Terry Pendleton, Dave Justice, are some of them and on your team Mark Grace, and Ryne Sandburg are all visually gifted to enable them to see slight offspeed changes," I responded.

He thought for a moment, "You are right. Those guys can rake. And they handle high-speed fastballs and all kinds of changes of speed pitches."

"Greg, I can watch hitters and after a while I can determine from observation if they have good speed recognition or not. For example, Wade Boggs, John Olerud, Roberto Alomar, Andres Galarraga are among the hitters that have great baseball-related visual skills that allow them to handle velocity pitches as well as a change of speed."

I then added, "Often hitters are like a driver driving down the highway. They look like they are looking. They look like they are paying attention, but they don't see what is directly in front of them. They end up sort of seeing the pitch fifteen to twenty feet after the ball is released. And, even at that, they often spin out and miss seeing the last 5-10 feet of a pitch."

It made sense to him that hitters generally did not track pitches deep enough, and that late break in pitches was very effective.

He spoke as if to no one but himself, "So they are not going to see a late break. Man, I will go to the bank with that insight."

He appeared to be getting excited, "What else?"

We proceeded to discuss how players would turn so much that their nose would block the eye away from the pitcher. I also pointed that in my evaluations of position players I was able to identify those that had poor "pitch speed awareness" and those that had good "pitch speed awareness." I pointed out that we provided training for those that did not have high quality "pitch speed awareness" or which we might call "velocity blindness."

He responded, "I know when I hit, I can often see the pitchers' pitches be released from slightly different release points. I can't necessarily hit them as often as I wish, but I can see the type of pitch."

"That is one of the ways experienced hitters, help themselves. They don't necessarily see the change of speed, but they recognize that the pitch coming from a different spot than the fastball is one that is going to be slower and have more trajectory change."

Over time, Greg became convinced that there weren't many hitters that could tell the speed of a pitch with any meaningful accuracy. We also talked about how hitters had imperceptions in their height judgment and by watching them from a perspective of "What were they seeing?" as well as observing their mechanical breakdowns would reveal some true visual holes in their hitting.

As he continued to think how to best disguise a pitch or

make them deceptive, Greg's primary goal was to "Make all of my pitches look like a rope coming toward home plate." Every pitch should look as close to every other as possible, all part of that "rope."

Regarding what hitters could see, Greg took it much further than our discussion in that he developed a mechanical approach that made it the toughest for hitters to see. He emphasized having all of his pitches leave from the same consistent release point and had multiple types of pitches with late break.

He made a great effort to master releasing each pitch from a consistent release point. As he honed the same release point, the same look, to all his pitches, all of his pitches started off looking the same.

At one time, Greg asked me, "What hitter in the National Leagues has the best eyes?"

I immediately responded, "I suspect it to be Barry Bonds." I had worked previously for a few years with the Pittsburgh Pirates, beginning in 1986 when Barry was a rookie and through the 1991 season.

A couple of years later in spring training, Greg approached me and said, "If Bonds has such great vision, what do I throw to him?" This was when Barry became a San Francisco Giants and I had no conflict of working with him.

I thought for a moment. I thought not one pitcher had asked me a question like this. I responded, "Change of pitches, change of speed just may not be enough. I suggest you change his eye level, with pitches above the strike zone or below the strike zone. The change of speeds still works, but you have to change the location maximally."

From then on he was very effective handling Bonds, as well as handling most hitters in the National League.

I think what Greg gained the most was a strengthening of his confidence that the most difficult thing for hitters to see was slight changes of speed of the same pitch. Syd Thrift and I each emphasized that a 3-5 mph change of speed of the same pitch was the most difficult thing for a hitter to see. Syd had seen it work so well with former pitchers we had worked with including Paul Splittorff, Dennis Leonard, Rick Rhoden and Rick Reuschel.

Greg began to gain confidence in the fact that hitters could not see slight changes of speed and when he didn't have his best stuff, knew that changing speeds during a game was often times more effective than trying to throw harder or make a pitch break more sharply.

He also capitalized on the fact of throwing the same pitch on the outside corner followed by a pitch the inside corner, or vice versa, was effectively chasing the speed 4-5 mph. He also understood that a fastball low and away compared to the same fastball high and inside, gave the hitter a different amount of time to react, because of the contact point the hitter needed in order to make contact.

We started a dialog that continued during his years with the Braves, through the 2003 season. Most of our discussions were based on what hitters could see and what they could not see.

We also talked a lot about golf, and I told him what PGA professionals like Gary Player, Jim Colbert, Fuzzy Zoeller, and others did to fine-tune their concentration. Greg probably could have helped golf professionals more than they could help him.

But he loved pitching. The challenge of pitching the pitch that the hitter wasn't looking for was a big part of his competitiveness. The master illusionist capitalized on deception. There is a famous illusion in which the viewer can see either an old woman or a young woman. It was as if Greg had hitters looking for the young woman when he would show them the old woman. They wouldn't see the young woman until it was too late.

Though I knew what he was doing, as a fan, it was incredible to me to see good major league hitters swing through balls, just missing them. What I was seeing was hitters swinging at a ball that was traveling 85mph and yet they saw it as if it was traveling at either 89mph or 81 mph. They could make contact at times but never squared the ball with great contact. He was simply an artist of visual illusions.

Greg was known for intensely studying hitters in preparation for his starts. He would often watch hitters take their warm-up swings or read their body language to gauge their mentality. He was credited by many of his teammates with a preternatural ability to outthink his opponents and anticipate results.

"From the dugout I have found if I look between the pitcher and the hitter, I can see when the hitter loads and gets his front foot down in relationship to the pitcher's release. Most guys are late, and once they see they ball they try to speed everything up. To me, I know I want to feed those guys off-speed pitches as a steady diet."

He went on, "I also look to see if guys are bailing out, leaving the outside of the strike zone as a great place for my pitch. I also see if they dive into an outside pitch, in which case I then want to come in on them."

I told him, "Greg if they are fouling the ball straight back to the catcher with foul tips, that means they are right on time, you should consider increasing or decreasing velocity on them."

We also discussed the need to follow is pitch all the way into the catcher's glove.

I suggested, "Greg you probably have learned in golf that if you track every ball you hit, what you see after it lands and bounces along will often tell you a lot about how you hit it. You will gain a sense of what you did right or wrong in terms of your swing mechanics."

"Yes, I have improved my golf game by doing just that," he replied.

"Well, the same is true in pitching. Don't give up on any pitch, because what you see will give you valuable feedback."

"That makes a lot of sense to me," he replied.

Within time, he got to where his work wasn't done once he pitched his intended pitch. He started with carefully tracking the ball when he threw in the bullpen. In games, when a batter took a ball or a strike, he kept his eyes on his catcher, perhaps as long as or longer than any pitcher. He didn't turn away immediately, he didn't drop his head. Rather, he looked for clues and solutions.

"I always visually replayed that pitch so I could see how the hitter reacted to that pitch, no matter whatever my pitch did," Maddux explained to me later. "The hitter's reaction always tells me all I need to know."

If the hitter nods his head, Maddux got to where he could read that as him seeing the pitch well. "I just watch that guy," Maddux said.

"I always watch hitters on the days I didn't pitch, during games and in batting practice. I look for where their hands are, whether their stances are open or closed, where the hitter stands in the box. "That all tells me what the hitter is trying to do, and what pitch they can handle," said Maddux.

Chapter 7

GREG MADDUX

Developing and Using a Personal Focusing Plan

You are going to learn about you can develop and use a Personal Focusing Plan assures that you think and focus before you act. It gives you total focus while you are performing. By always using this strategy, you will enjoy higher self-confidence, control, and poise. You will find that composure and self-control will be your habitual manner of acting. You will stop trying to arrive at that state and will find yourself just being there naturally. There always becomes a moment you must pitch effectively and with a purpose. At this point, there's no time for another team meeting to evaluate the opponent or to recite a mantra. You have to pitch effectively, often times when all the chips are on the table. It's too late for more analysis; forget the alternatives, now is the time to just do it. Your Personal Performance Focusing Plan will guide you and allow you to do it effectively.

When I first met Greg in 1992, he had already established himself as a very good pitcher. He didn't really need to get any better.

In the prior 6 seasons, he had a 74-64 with an earned run average of around 3.50. At age 22 he had a remarkable 18-2 record with a 3.18 era. In 1989 at age 23, he was 19-12 with a 2.94 era. It was a fantastic record for anyone pitching for the Chicago Cubs and in Wrigley Field where few had succeeded for a very long period.

One day in 1992 spring training in the Cubs Clubhouse at

Fitch Park in Mesa, Arizona, Greg Maddux and I, after talking about reading putts, shifted to talking about having a consistent progression of focus on each pitch, no matter what the game conditions were at the time

Greg said, "I think if I have a more consistent approach, my mechanics will be more consistent and I will have better pitch command.

Jamie Moyer, Bob Scanlan, Mike Morgan and young minor league pitcher Steve Trachsel were nearby.

Some coaches thought Jamie Moyer's pitching career was over. He had pitched part of six seasons in the Major Leagues and had an unremarkable 34-55 record

32-year-old Mike Morgan had come over from Los Angeles Dodgers. At that time, he had pitched 11 seasons in the big leagues as he broke in with Oakland at age 18 as a no. 1 draft choice. With the Dodgers in 3 seasons he was 33-36

Scanlan, a 28th round draft choice by the Philadelphia Phillies, was a 25-year-old and had pitched for the Cubs the prior season.

The initial discussion about reading putts occurred because Greg learned that I was working with PGA Golf Pro Jim Colbert. Colbert was based out of Las Vegas, Greg's home, so Greg knew quite a bit about him. At that time, Jim was winning a lot of tournaments on the Senior PGA Golf Tour.

I told Greg, knowing other pitchers were listening, "Jim Colbert had a tendency to get too mechanical when the chips were on the table. Invariably he wouldn't play well when the pressure was on. So we worked on a focusing progression, a personal focus plan, which has helped Jim stay more visual, less mechanical. As a result, he has begun to play much better."

Mike Morgan asked, "How did you come up with this?"

"Jim told me he needed a repeatable system to keep his

focus on each golf shot. One day Jim said to me 'Bill, am starting to understand what you are saying, and I really like this visual flow perspective, but how do I put it into play?'"

Mike said, "All of us pitchers need that."

I told him, "I am going to give you four steps to follow." Keeping the discussion on golf, I said, "I suggest you do it on every shot, not just when you feel like you are in trouble."

I went on knowing I was getting the various pitcher's attention, "The first step is to analyze. It is important that you take a moment to see, feel and think about the upcoming shot."

"But you must analyze and not anal-ize. You analyze quickly and move on to the next step. Do not continue to analyze."

Scanlan pitched in, "Okay. I do know I overdue it often. And I tend to anal-ize and not analyze."

"The second step is to visualize what you plan your intended result to be. See it and feel yourself producing that result. For example, in golf it is important that it is a visualization of what you have decided to be the shot you want to hit. In this manner, it doesn't allow for a picture of a mistake, a mechanical flaw or something you don't want to do, such as hit the ball into a trap. In that instance, it has to be a picture of hitting the ball onto the green."

Seeing the connection of golf to pitching Mike Morgan offered "I do that all the time. I picture not making a mistake. And when I do that is exactly what happens."

I then headed rapidly toward a conclusion because I didn't want to lose their interest by saying "Now, the third step is to center on the task at hand. It's really a sequence of centering from the begging moment to the time to execute your shot. It includes one hundred percent attention on the back of the ball at the moment of hitting it."

I looked around at the various guys in the training room,

"The next step is to execute. You execute by letting it happen and not making it happen."

Scanlan said, "I like that a lot."

Morgan laughed as he said, "So are you saying we need to AVCEX on each pitch?"

I laughed along with the pitchers and said, "Yes, AVCEX whenever you need to perform."

After more laughter I added, "So if we take the first letter of each word we end up with an acronym that says AVCEX. I recommended to Colbert that he needed to AVCEX on every single golf shot. The consistency of the visual sequence of thought will result in greater consistency in your performance. We'll tweak each step so that you can maximize each step, but the key is using them all together in a flowing sequence."

Maddux said, "I can see this helping me on the golf course. I sometimes only analyze and am still analyzing as I try to hit the shot. The results are never good. I sometimes get caught up in just seeing the picture of a golf shot and don't move on to doing it. I think the system will help my thought processes flow and be complete prior to each shot."

Greg paused and then said, "This directly relates to pitching."

As we further discussed the AVEX Loop, I added another thought "One more thing. To get proficient and getting the benefit from AVCEX Loop, I want you to begin the habit of doing a complete replay of what you just did. Do it after each shot."

I paused for emphasis and then said, "In other words, you AVCEX, you hit your shot or putt, and then you review just how you analyzed, visualized, centered and executed. Your replay is going to tell you exactly what you did. At times, you will find that your centering slipped. At other times, you will find the right pattern, the right sequence and be happy with the result."

I paused again for emphasis, "Within time you will be able to repeat the proper formula, your AVCEX Loop formula, to consistently hit high-quality shots."

Bob Scanlan said, "And to consistently pitch high-quality pitches." I wanted to hug Scanlan for making that connection.

Greg responded, "If this works as well as I think it will in my golf game, I am sure going to utilize it when I pitch."

Syd Thrift walked into the clubhouse and came over. I looked up and said to him, "Syd we are all talking about the need to AVCEX."

He chuckled for a moment and then said, "Guys this is a very effective approach. In fact, it is something you would want to use in a lot of things you do. I try to AVCEX all the time."

The pitchers cracked up.

Scanlan said, "Doc, how did you come up with this. How did you now it would help Jim Colbert?"

I responded, "It just sort of came together. I do think my military experience had something to do with it. We were very interested in helping soldiers observe better and be better focused on what they were doing."

Scanlan quizzed, "How is observation so necessary for a soldier?"

I spoke up, "Yes, Bob, intent observation is a significant part of a well-accepted military strategy known as the OODA Loop."

Jamie Moyer spoke up, "What is that all about? I've got a belt loop. Does that qualify?" Again, the various guys in the clubhouse were laughing

I paused because a couple of other young pitchers came

into the training room. I went on, "The OODA Loop is a learning system and decision-making process that was laid out by Air Force fighter pilot and military strategist John Boyd."

I paused and looked around at each pitcher, "The four steps Boyd felt a fighter pilot should use was to Observe, Orient, Decide, and Act. He called it the OODA Loop."

One of the young minor league pitchers asked, "Fighter pilot? What are you guys talking about?"

Knowing that I wasn't going to fully answer his question, I said "In a head-to-head competition, like air-to-air combat, a violent confrontation in a parking lot, and the person who can cycle through the OODA Loop the fastest usually wins."

Young Trachsel spoke up and said, "This is great stuff. I love fighting. In fact, I always wanted to be a fighter pilot."

I commented, "Fighter pilots are known for battling for their lives in dogfights. The OODA loop was developed to assure fast, accurate and repeatable performance actions."

Not wanting to push the idea toward pitching, while recognizing these guys would make their own connection, I offered, "As a golfer or like piloting a fighter jet, a dogfight is frequently involved. In each fight you must: Outmaneuver the competition, respond decisively to fast-changing conditions, and defeat your rivals."

Maddux said, "That fits me. I often feel like I am in a dogfight."

Then he said, "I can see how this fits Jim Colbert and his AVCEXing approach."

Chuck McElroy had just come into the clubhouse. Chuck broke up with laughter, "AVCEXing? What the heck does that have to do with playing golf?"

I looked around at the various pitchers, knowing that I would get their full attention I asked rather boldly, "How many of you guys are AVCEXing on the mound?"

Everyone was laughing, and I know they were likely thinking something like, 'What is it with this nut case?'"

Greg said, "Tell these guys that just walked in what AVCEX is all about."

I went on talking knowing the new guys were listening, "The first step is to analyze. It is important that you take a moment to see, feel and think about the upcoming golf shot."

Scanlan asked, "Or pitch?" I nodded to him in agreement.

Greg pitched in with a wry smile, "But as you told me you must analyze and not anal-ize. You analyze quickly and move on to the next step. Do not continue to analyze, because over-analyzing turns into anal-izing." A lot of laughter ensued.

Scanlan pitched in, "Okay. I know I tend to anal-ize and not analyze. I do it in golf and I do it too often when I pitch."

I then repeated describing AVCEX, "The second step is to visualize what you plan your intended result to be. This is when you see it and feel yourself producing that effect. It is important that it is a visualization of what you have decided to be the shot you want to hit. In this manner, it doesn't allow for a picture of a mistake, a mechanical flaw or something you don't want to do, such as hit the ball into a trap. In that instance, it has to be a picture of hitting the ball onto the green."

One young pitcher offered "I do that all the time. I picture not making a mistake. And when I do that it is what happens."

Keeping the discussion on golf, I quickly added, "When you visualize a golf shot correctly you should sense a flow of energy producing that shot."

Moyer offered, "There is nothing quite like the feeling of a great golf shot."

Again keeping the discussion on golf, I added, "Now, the third step is to center on the task at hand. It's a sequence of centering from the beginning moment through the time to execute the shot. You have a flowing focus progression. This is the time you lock in. This is similar to the Action step in John Boyd's OODA Loop."

I looked around at the various guys in the training room, all of whom seemed to be listening, "The next step is to execute. You execute by letting it happen and not making it happen."

Morgan said, "I like that a lot."

In an attempt to summarize I added, "So as I said, if we take the first letter of each word we end up with an acronym that says AVCEX. I recommended to Colbert that he needed to AVCEX on every single golf shot. The consistency of the visual flow sequence of thought will result in greater consistency in your performance. We'll tweak each step so that you can maximize each step, but the key is using them all together in a flowing sequence."

Morgan said, "I can see this helping me on the golf course. I sometimes only analyze and am still analyzing as I try to hit the shot. The results are never good. I sometimes get caught up in just seeing the picture of a golf shot and don't move on to doing it. I think the system will help my thought processes flow and be complete prior to each shot."

Scanlan said, "You mentioned that military strategy called the OODA Loop. I understand the Observation, Decision, and Action steps, but what is the Orient all about."

"Good question, Bob," I responded. "Orientation is best understood if you imagine look in your garage and find among other things, skis, outboard motor, handlebars and rubber treads."

"Imagine what emerges when you put these particular parts together. Can you figure it out?"

Greg Maddux said, "It's a snowmobile." Maddux's intellect, on and off the mound, was very impressive.

"You are entirely correct Greg. Orienting, in a nutshell, is the ability to make figurative mental snowmobiles on the fly and in the face of uncertainty. In reality, it is about your thoughts many that are visual in nature. Some call it this a mental model."

Scanlan said, "Strategy of being in a dogfight makes sense."

I took his thought further and added, "John Boyd, the developer of the OODA Loop concept was quoted to say, 'We gotta get an image or picture in our head, which we call orientation. Then we have to make a decision as to what we're going to do and then implement the decision. Then we look at the resulting action, plus our observation, and we drag in new data, new orientation, new decision, new action, ad infinitum.'"

As we further discussed the AVCEX Loop, I added another thought "One more thing. To really get proficient and getting the benefit from AVCEX Loop or the OODA Loop, I suggest you begin the habit of doing a complete replay of what you just did. Do it after each shot. In other words, you AVCEX, you hit your shot or putt, and then you review just how you analyzed, visualized, centered and executed. Your replay is going to tell you exactly what you did. At times, you will find that your centering slipped. At other times, you will find the right pattern, the right sequence and be happy with the result. Within time you will be able to repeat the proper formula, your AVCEX Loop formula, to hit consistently high-quality shots."

Morgan said, "Okay Doc. We have to run. We are in a golf tournament, and we have a tee time an hour from now. I am going to be sure and AVCEX today."

The next day in the clubhouse, Morgan was beaming again. "We all played our best golf yesterday. I played with

Maddux, Moyer, and McElroy. We were the 4 M's." He smiled, "They played each played better than normal."

Maddux walked in and after overhearing what we were talking about he offered, "It seems like we were focused on each shot. I know in my case I didn't find myself over-thinking, I just made a plan and followed it. I hit a few poor shots, but all in all, I hit a lot of quality shots."

"Do you think you can AVCEX when you pitch?"

Greg quickly responded, "Without a doubt. It will definitely help me pitch one pitch at a time."

Some minor league pitchers came in the clubhouse and I could tell they were confused and a bit shocked to hear my strange question to Greg so I added one final comment to Greg, "It doesn't make any difference whether you choose to use AVCEX or the OODA Loop, you need a system to follow that incorporates everything you might need on a pitch. In a simple way think in terms you want a consistent way to plan, act and learn on each pitch."

I paused and then said, "You should analyze, visualize, center and execute on each of your pitches in your pre-bullpen thoughts, in the bullpen, and in the game."

Greg smiled and said, "Well, I'll leave the OODA Loop to the military. I'm going to get good at AVCEXing then."

I looked around and several young pitchers were standing and sort of observing and listening in awe. Among them were Shawn Boskie, Turk Wendell, Lance Dickson, Heathcliff Slocumb, Blaise Isley and Kennie Steenstra. After all, Maddux was the Cubs proven ace and these guys were hoping to make the team's roster and go "North" with the team.

I quickly looked at each of them and gave a quick capsulation of what I told Maddux, Morgan, Moyer, McElroy and Scanlan.

"Guys, in a nutshell, what were talking about is the

importance of developing a consistent routine, you might want to call it a process, but it is your personal performance plan and focusing plan." I paused to see if I had their attention.

Turk spoke up and asked, "How do we do it?"

"In games, prior to each pitch, you very quickly analyze the game conditions. This includes what you know about your pitches actions, what you have seen from the hitter. You should do this quickly. At some point, you should take a deep breath. Then after you see your catcher's sign, you visualize and feel the trajectory of your pitch doing directly through your intended target," I paused again to see if they were following along.

"Then, you should center your full attention on a specific target and once you see your target clearly, you should then execute your pitch. At this point you let it happen, don't try to make it happen."

Lance Dickson, "This is great stuff. I wish I would have known this before." Lance was trying to recover from a career-ending arm injury. Unfortunately, he never recovered

"So the idea here is you do this on every pitch. It will help you pitch one pitch at a time. You need to think about it. You need to apply it consciously in the bullpen. And then pitch in games following this regimen."

Syd Thrift had walked up in the background and then he spoke up.

"Guys let's get out on the field. There is a lot of AVCEXing we need to be doing today." The young guys totally howled with laughter.

I concluded with advising the young pitchers to begin writing down the elements that they thought they each could use in their own Personal Focusing Plan. I encouraged that it is a plan that will unique to each of them and will evolve over as a result of your own experiences.

"In a few days we will get together and go over various elements you may want to use," I added.

As an aside each of these young pitchers were called up from the minor leagues within the next season or two and enjoyed a major league career.

From time to time I have thought, "Would the Chicago Cubs pitchers had as much success as they did if they hadn't learned what we initially developed at the Kansas City Royals Baseball Academy and the concepts that were proven by Mark Littell and Paul Splittorff?"

Perhaps Ewing Kauffman, Syd Thrift, Mark Littell, Steve Blass, and Paul Splittorff were a big part of various pitcher's success and long-time careers.

In 1992, Mike Morgan went 16-8 with a .255 era, arguably the best season of his 22-year career in which he ended up 141-186.

Turk Wendell made the show in 1993 and enjoyed 11 years as a premier reliever for the Cubs, Mets, and Phillis.

Jamie Moyer was released at the end of spring training. He signed on with the Detroit Tigers and pitched for Toledo in AAA and was 10-8 with a 380 ERA. He returned to the MLB with Baltimore in 1993, pitched 19 more years and ended up 269-205. He actually went a remarkable 235-150 after the 1992 spring training.

Bob Scanlan was a 25th round drafted by the Philadelphia Phillies in 1984. He came up with the Cubs in 1991 and posted a 7-8 with one save. In 1992, he had his most effective year in a nine-year career as he had a 2.89 era and 14 saves as a reliever finished 41 games each were the highest of his career.

Steve Trachsel, a 21-year-old, pitched at Charlotte in AA that year and went 13-8. The next year, at 22, he pitched at Iowa and went 13-6 and was called up at the end of the season. He ended up pitched for 16 years in the major leagues with a 143-159 won-loss record.

Chuck McElroy had pitched part of the three prior seasons. He became a regular reliever in 1992 was a very effective mid-game left-handed reliever who pitched 13 seasons in the major leagues.

In 1992, he closed 30gamesand saved 6 the highest of his career.

Greg Maddux took it up a notch in 1992, winning the Cy Young Award as he went 20-11with a 2.18 era. Joining the Braves in 1993, a winning team, he then went 20-22, 10-20, and 19-2 in the next 3 seasons with an era under .200. 4 Cy Young Awards in a row was an extraordinary achievement. He went on to pitch for 23 seasons and had a 355-227 lifetime record with a 3.16 era. What was the Chicago Cubs ownership at that time thinking? 1982 Greg was already making $4.2M and the Braves offered were able to sign him in 1993 for $5,875M. Rightfully he made nearly $155 Million over his 23 seasons. He definitely executed a very good plan.

How2Focus: **The Pitchers Zone**

Chapter 8

The Great Glavine, Maddux, Smoltz Led Atlanta Braves Pitching Staff

After Greg Maddux's great year in 1992 with the Chicago Cubs, he not only won the Cy Young Award but he signed a long time contract with the Atlanta Braves. With the Braves, he joined 1991 Cy Young Award winner Tom Glavine and future winner John Smoltz. All became Hall of Fame inductees. They led what could be considered the <u>most accomplished starting trio</u> ever assembled on a single Major League team. Smoltz could do it all—basketball, golf, and pitch. You will learn Glavine was almost as good. As great as they were they learned a lot about pitching from their new teammate Maddux. Golf provided a common ground and not only was recreational but was educational as they learned about themselves and their best way to compete. In this chapter, you will learn the same insights on how to develop an effective focusing plan and how it relates to how military fighter pilots used an effective focusing loop to keep themselves effective. Maddux, Smoltz, and Glavine pitched in the zone—nearly every outing. You will gain insights into a focusing plan that gets you into a visual flow which leads you to the zone. You will learn how the 'zone' has taken on an aura, much greater and more mysterious than its true nature. You will see that the zone is not something remote and magical and associated only with superstars at their best. But in reality, the zone is nothing more than extended periods of peak efficiency, of which we are all capable. You will gain the insight that visual alertness, focus, and concentration are characteristics of the visual flow. You will learn a method that allows you to correct on-the-spot decisions are made, awareness is enlarged or magnified, and sensory cues are much more sensitive and accurate.

I began working with the Atlanta Braves in 1991. I had spent the prior two seasons working just with various Braves position players—Terry Pendleton, Ron Gant, Dave Justice, Otis Nixon, Jeff Blauser, Greg Olson, Rafael Belliard, Mark Lemke and Tommy Gregg.

I was fortunate to see Greg's during his first day in 1973 with the Atlanta Braves in the training room at Spring Training in West Palm Beach, Florida. He was now a very financially secure young man, but I could see he hadn't changed at all. He was the same old Greg.

From day one he was well received by various Braves star pitchers including John Smoltz and Tommy Glavine.

I had seen how Greg had a significant impact on the other pitchers on the Cubs staff, as he was almost like an extra coach. I was sure that he would have the same effect on the Braves pitching staff, even Smoltz, and Glavine. I knew he would convey to his teammates his beliefs about preparation, mechanics, strategy, observing hitters, focus, handling adversity, learning from the situation and how to improve their performance.

Though I had met and observed John Smoltz and Tommy Glavine in the prior two seasons Greg introduced me to each of them.

Greg said, "Bill has a lot to offer our pitching staff." I could tell that they didn't have much of an understanding of how that could be true. They thought I was just helping the position players see the ball better.

Glavine had a great 1991 season. Tommy at age 26 was a six-year veteran had just come off of two 20 winning games seasons. He had been 73-50 in his first six years and was the 1991 Cy Young Award winner and was runner-up to Maddux in 1992.

Smoltz had been 67-54 in his prior 5 seasons but was not yet in the Glavine or Maddux level. His career started forward in 1996 when he had his best season in as when he went 24-8 and took the Cy Young Award away from Maddux

I was not planning to talk to John or Tommy on anything about pitching, but I was aware they loved playing golf almost as much as he loved pitching.

One spring training in West Palm Beach, I overheard Greg telling a number of pitchers including Glavine and Smoltz, "If you look down a road, it is was impossible to tell if a car was going 55, 65 or 75 mph unless there was another car nearby to offer a point of reference.

"You just can't do it," he said. "Sometimes hitters can pick up differences in spin. They can identify pitches if there are different releases points or if a curveball starts with an upward hump as it leaves the pitcher's hand. But if a pitcher can change speeds, every hitter is helpless, limited by human vision.

Prior to my working with professional pitchers on the visual and mental sides of the game, I had worked with position players and I spent considerable time with professional golfers. In working with PGA Tour golfers Jim Colbert, Fuzzy Zoeller, Butch Baird, Don Iverson, Dale Douglass, Jim Weichers, John Schroeder, Billy Casper, and a young friend of Colbert's, Payne Stewart, I became convinced that the mental requirements of a pitcher and a golfer were very similar.

John was always hanging out in the trainer's room. Glavine was not very visible. He came late and left early. Later that spring, when I was around John I would try to stir up a conversation about his golf game. Usually, his golf partners Maddux and Glavine were nearby and the conversation had started by "Where are we playing today?"

My opinion is that golf is a fantastic sport for pitchers to play and attempt to develop proficiency. A golfer and a pitcher have complete control of their situations. They each can take an appropriate time to prepare for their actions. They each can see what happened as a result of their actions, and they can make any adjustment that they deem necessary prior to their next action. The most common factor is that they each need a consistent focus progression that allows them to lock in for their respective actions. Also, they each benefit from getting into a focused flow that takes them in the proverbial zone. And in both instances, they must each always be learning.

My visual performance ideas in golf were well received, and several golfers went on to win their first PGA Tournaments after employing the visual side of the game — Baird, Iverson, Wiechers, and Schroeder were among them.

At various tournament sites, I had the opportunity to bounce my ideas off of several veteran winners — Bruce Devlin, David Graham, and a big star Gary Player.

Gary Player told me that he once had a vision in the British Open when he arrived before the event started on Monday. He saw himself holding the Claret Jug, later calling it a a Deja vu experience. He ended up winning on Sunday.

Player, in fact, looked me in the eye and said, "Bill, be very careful who you talk to about these vision and visualization ideas. Visualization is very, very powerful. And with power comes danger. Be careful who you talk to about visualization."

I had to think about that for some time. It did indicate to me that Gary Player had used his visual thinking skills very successfully himself. I also gained the sense that since it was so helpful to him, he didn't want other guys he was competing against to know much about it.

One day in 1994, Greg and I were talking about the importance of observation for a pitcher. Mike Bielecki, who I became acquainted with when I was working for and he was a young Pittsburgh Pirates pitcher at the time. This was the first year with the Braves for the 34-year-old right-hander.

"Bi" as he was known joined in on the discussions, walked into the athletic trainer's room and overhead what Greg and Mike were talking about. Ironically he didn't say anything. He just listened as athletic trainer David Pursley began working on his shoulder.

Bi said to Greg, "You can pitch while wearing a blindfold. Why are you talking to Harrison?" He looked at me and winked.

Greg said, "Seeing well is a major part of my game. I've learned that I can't just let a pitch go and forget it. I've found that seeing the late action of my pitch helped me a lot. It helped me realize that when my pitched didn't move as I intended I needed to make an adjustment with my pitching mechanics."

Bielecki said, "Greg, are you telling me you can see your pitch's action as it passes through the contact zone?"

Maddux went on, "For sure. Most importantly, while watching the pitch flight carefully, I could see the opposing hitter's reaction. I could see when they were diving toward the outside of the plate, I could see when they were slightly late, slightly early and when they were more on their heels likely looking for an inside pitch."

Greg said, "Observation is an important factor for me whether I'm on the golf course or the pitching mound." I sensed Greg wanted Bielecki to hear some of his beliefs

I added, "So you observe, and then you attack their weakness or openings."

Greg said "Yes. Those hitters are my enemy when I am on the mound. I want to see everything they do and I almost always find a way to conquer them."

With the pitches which I did not know or had a prior relationship with as I had had with Maddux and Bielecki, I have to admit I had a strategy. With these successful veteran pitchers, including Smoltz and Glavine, my strategy was not to tell them of any of my thoughts about pitching. I only talked about golf, but my strategy was to discuss aspects of golf that I thought they might connect to pitching.

Smoltz, Maddux and I talked about target selection in various golf shots. I suggested that on a putt they could actually see one blade of grass on the side of the cup that they wanted the ball to roll into the hole.

Greg said, "I like pitching to small spots, so putting to a very small spot makes sense."

I emphasize that taking the time to visualize a golf shot did multiple helpful things, but one was it helped placed a higher level focus on the final target.

One day John after asking him about his golf game the day before he said to me, "I have been missing my short putts, one after another."

I said, "John try some for me today. As you are over the putt, initially look to see where you want the ball to end up and then slowly trace a line from that spot back to the ball."

I paused as he was thinking how he could do that, "You can do it more than once, perhaps two or three times on certain difficult putts."

I could tell he liked the idea after he thought him through.

The next day he came into the clubhouse and it was apparent he had played well the day before, He said, "thanks, I took everyone's money yesterday. My putts were spot on."

He said, "Can that be helpful in pitching."

"Sure it can," I responded. "In fact, several years ago I

was introduced to Bert Blyleven. Bert told me he couldn't throw a waste pitch high and inside to a right-handed hitter."

I paused and said, "So I encouraged him to look directly at the small area that he wanted the high and tight pitch to go. Then I told him to see the pitch come backward ten to fifteen feet and then back to his small target in the catcher's glove."

John said, "That sounds like a good idea. I know I can use that."

From that day on we talked about how he saw his putts, but also his pitches.

Another time he was bemoaning his golf game and asked him a few questions. It was clear to me he was over-thinking.

Manager Bobby Cox was revered by his players. The pitchers really appreciated that he would have them get their work done and then could get off the field, at least an hour earlier than the position players. As the pitchers completed their bullpen sessions, usually two at a time, they would come in the athletic trainer's room to get various treatments.

One day in 1996 several pitchers were wearing ice packs on their shoulders in the training room. Maddux, John Smoltz, Tom Glavine, and Steve Avery had finished their on the field workouts and were killing time though Maddux was getting a massage on his lower back.

Glavine was always quiet around me. I never knew what he was thinking, but I did get the sense that he was listening. I also know he and Smoltz were always asking Maddux his opinion about various things he saw in hitter's reactions that tipped on how to get the guy out.

Of all the Braves pitchers, John Smoltz was the greatest conversationalist. When he was in the training room, we mainly talked about golf. But when John talked most of the other pitcher just listened.

But we also talked about what I called the visual flow,

and he called "the zone." John had his own distinct opinion about things. My intent was not to change his opinion but to get him looking at other possibilities.

Frankly, we argued a bit because our views were a little different initially. My emphasis was that he could control the visual flow. Furthermore, I emphasized that there were levels of visual flow, but he could learn to do it on practice days and then do the same thing when he was playing a round.

I suggested, "John, your eyes and your brain-based vision can slow down what you see. Once things look slow, your brain relaxes and based on your level of arousal you will fall in the zone. When you are just pitching in the bullpen, because you are not aroused as you are when you pitch in a game, it may not seem to be exactly like being in the zone, because you don't have all the brain chemistry being active as when you pitch in a game. But you can pitch in the bullpen free of body awareness, free of thoughts, visually focused and just let it happen. If you do so, it will within time pitching in some level of the zone become a habit."

John kept talking about how great it was when he got into the zone. I sensed he didn't fully buy into what I told him. At the same time, I knew when he heard Maddux say essentially the same, he would then buy in

I did say, "I think a better name for the zone is 'the visual flow' or being 'in the visual flow.' Since most people believe that the zone is just a random visit of a special grace, those sudden hot streaks, those unexpected displays of rare excellence, took on an air of great mystery."

I could see he was beginning to think about what I had said and then said "John, I believe you can set the stage for visual flow experiences to occur and have access to it all the time."

"If so, that would be very powerful," John commented as he looked around the room at other young pitchers who were just listening.

I explained further to John that the 'visual flow' is where things start clicking. It was sort of like getting on an automatic pilot of elevated performance and that it can happen during any activity, mental or physical. For most people, getting into the visual flow is very infrequent, a random happening that just appears out of nowhere. And it disappears just as suddenly. But for those who wish to look deeper than surface reality, a fertile field exists, a field where the visual flow is always available to who know to cultivate it."

"That's for me. I want to be able to call it up, at will," John said in a rather loud voice.

I emphasized that visual alertness is a characteristic of visual flow. It allows for correct on-the-spot decisions are made, awareness is enlarged or magnified and sensory cues are much more sensitive and accurate.

We agreed that being 'zone' had been popularized greatly by the sports media, and, as so often happen with buzzwords and catchphrases. It has taken on an aura, much greater and more mysterious than its true nature. The average sports fan considers the zone to be something remote and magical and associates it only with superstars at their best. But in reality, the zone is nothing more than extended periods of peak efficiency, of which we are all capable.

Within time and without a question John mastered the ability to get into the visual flow and if he got out of it, he could quickly recover and get back into it. He had command of the zone when he pitched, particularly in big games of the postseason.

I think the golf connection was very important with the great Braves pitching staff. I am a believer that you can learn how to perform at your craft by learning from people who are proficient at doing other crafts.

Golf has always seemed to be somewhat similar to baseball. Most people think of that statement in relation to the baseball swing. However, I think the parallel with golf is with pitching. Each requires intense focus and careful, consistent preparation to perform well.

Once I recall John saying "Mentally, golf and pitching were perfect for allowing me to stay sharp and use the things I had as a pitcher to my advantage as a golfer."

Later John told me "Most of my complete games came the day after I played golf. It was unbelievable how mentally freed up I felt after playing golf. If I could have gotten away with it, and there wouldn't have been such a media frenzy, I probably would have played nine or 18 holes the day I pitched. I loved playing golf, being loose and exercising and rotating and getting everything the way it needed to be."

I don't know how much of what was discussed was used by John in his pitching. But I do know he used the ideas in golf that improved his capability on the golf course and likely he used the relevant ideas on the mound.

John was great, but I do think part of his success was due to what he learned about the mental approach to the game from Greg Maddux.

The Braves pitching staff was not only the best pitching staff in the 1990's but arguably one of the best pitching staffs of all time.

From time to time I have thought, "Would the great Atlanta Braves pitching staff had as much success as they did if they hadn't learned what we initially developed at the Kansas City Royals Baseball Academy and the concepts that were proven by Mark Littell and Paul Splittorff?"

Perhaps Ewing Kauffman, Mark Littell, Steve Blass, and Paul Splittorff were a big part of various Atlanta Braves' pitcher's success. They certainly capitalized on Greg Maddux's performance knowledge.

Chapter 9

Jason Johnson
A Big Career U-turn

You will learn how a young MLB pitcher with a 1-10 record and a 7.02 ERA turned his career around after learning how to focus, use off the field focusing drills, to regain his role as an MLB starter. You will gain insights on the importance of defining your task at hand and committing to that task, no matter the game conditions. You will learn how this young pitcher made an abrupt change in his attitude of being totally confused about what he was doing on the mound to being happy with his performance. You will learn about some of the methods he used to refine his focus. You will gain further insights on the benefit of allowing your subconscious to take over when you pitch while just being conscious of your target. You will learn from the comments of a young pitcher, "It was one of those situations last year where I didn't think anything would help," Jason Johnson said. "I heard everything. I saw everything. This year, none of that occurred and I now have an entirely different attitude." Jason ended up with a 12 year MLB pitching career.

2000 was a terrible year for Jason Johnson. Once considered one of the Baltimore Orioles' most promising pitchers, he became an enigma. Jason had a live arm, could pitch a high-speed bullet, but could not locate his pitches.

And the Orioles suffered as they needed Jason to be an effective starting pitcher as they finished 4th in the American League Eastern Division. The team was loaded with seasoned veterans including Cal Ripken, Will Clark, Harold

Baines, B. J. Surhoff, Brady Anderson, Mike Bordick, Delino DeShields, Charles Johnson and Albert Belle. These guys were used to winning and it wasn't happening.

He lost his first eight decisions and finished the season 0-8 as a starter. In 107 2/3 innings, he allowed 17 stolen bases, a testament not only to his slow delivery as well as his distracted approach.

Jason ended up with a 1-10 record, 7.02 ERA, two options to Triple-A Rochester and a career's worth of self-doubt. He seemed to hit bottom shortly after being recalled from the minors for the second time in August 2000.

Later he said, "I felt totally lost and out of control. I had no idea of how to have success," he said. "I have to admit, I focused totally on my pitching mechanics. I left my focus to pure chance, as I had no idea it was that important to me.

A year later he looked and was an entirely different pitcher.

"It was one of those situations last year where I didn't think anything would help," Johnson said. "I heard everything. I saw everything. This year, none of that occurred, and I now have an entirely different attitude."

The turn-about when my friend of over twenty years, Syd Thrift, the then Baltimore Orioles Director of Personnel asked Johnson to fly to California a couple of days prior to the Orioles three-game series with the Angels in early September. Syd asked Jason to spend a day with me.

Jason was very skeptical, but he opened himself to give Syd's recommendation a chance. "When they first introduced me to the guy, I didn't know. But it was one of those things you had to give a chance. I did. And it's done a lot for me," Johnson was quoted later.

Initially, Jason and I talked about his career, and I finally got to how he had pitched in 2000 in Rochester.

Johnson did not struggle in his time at Rochester. He said, "The pressures were less in Rochester. I knew there was no way I could go any further down. There was no pressure," he said. "When I was in Baltimore, I was always worried about what would happen if my next start were a bad one."

His fear became self-fulfilling. Johnson never won a start last season nor did he win at home, a lone win coming in relief against the Tampa Bay Devil Rays.

"I'd hear everything going on around me," he said. "I couldn't tune anything out, so everything affected me. You can't succeed like that."

I reviewed with Jason various ideas on centering and pre-pitch feeling and seeing the pitch that had worked for Mark Littell, Paul Splittorff, Orel Hershiser, Greg Maddux, and others. I also went over in depth why it didn't work as effectively with Steve Blass.

In the course of a day and a half, we discussed a lot of topics to boil it all down to a simplified approach that he could implement.

At one point, I had Jason participate in a series of eye control drills.

I told Jason, "These drills are based on the performance concept of Follow Your Eyes as they will lead your body."

I then told him "If you are going to follow your eyes, you must control your eyes."

I then had him do some of my drills on a mini-trampoline. Jason did it remarkably well. Doing this drill takes considerable focus as well as ability to integrate the body with the eyes and with one's thoughts. It's a remarkable task of athletic concentration ability. After all, if an athlete can concentrate when he is sitting down, it doesn't mean he can concentrate when his body is in motion.

As we completed a lengthy drill, he said, "Doc, I was locked. It reminds me of how I felt when I was in the zone. I only focused on what you told me to be my task at hand. I don't remember what my body was doing. Was I okay?"

"You were great! You followed your eyes to get you in the zone. You let it happen. You didn't make it happen. You got out of your body's way and just let it perform."

Then I added, "That's what eye control can do for you."

"That's the way I want to be when I pitch," He added.

"Jason, when you have eye control, you control your brain and your body. When you pitch, keep your eyes riveted on your targets. Switch your eyes at will and control them you will be able to command yourself and your pitches."

I concluded that Jason was inherently gifted with great skill-sets.

Later the next season, Jason said to me "You asked me a question that really got my attention." he said. After my asking which question he replied, "You asked me what I thought my task was when I pitched."

"At first, I thought it was a simple answer. However, my initial thoughts were pretty scattered. I thought it was to win the game, to get guys out, to prevent runs, and thoughts like that. And then I thought and added, my task is to execute my mechanics correctly."

I recall much of that discussion when I responded, "None of those will the job done. They are not your task, Jason. They are your various goals. They are important, but they are not going to help you how to get it done."

I recall that he got quiet, obviously thinking, but not coming up with a better answer.

I had said to him, "Jason, your task is something that is your task no matter the game conditions. Your task is the same no matter the score. It is the same no matter how many men are on base. And it is the same no matter who it is that is hitting. It could be Babe Ruth or Humpty Dumpty; you want to be totally focused on pitching effectively to your task at hand."

"What's that?" he responded.

"Your task is no more or no less than the following," I paused. "Your task at hand is always to throw a quality pitch to a specific target."

I think that is when I got his attention. As simple as it was, he likely had never previously looked at pitching in that manner.

"And that specific target may be out of the strike zone at

times," I added.

After some time for him to think about it, I asked, "Can you do that? Can you throw a quality pitch to a specific target?"

"Sure I can," he quickly responded.

"Well, that is what you should be focused upon when you pitch in games. You need to do that on every pitch in a game whether you pitch one inning or nine innings. Your task is always the same."

"That makes total sense," he agreed.

So to get him thinking further I said, "Jason have you thrown various quality pitches to specific targets in the past?" I was attempting to get him to think more about his past pitching success.

"Sure, I have, lots of them," he replied.

"What did you do to make those pitches?" I inquired.

He thought and basically said he analyzed the situation, visualized and felt the pitch he wanted to throw, focused on a specific target and let it happen.

"So Jason, right now if the game was on the line and a team's best left-handed hitter coming up, can you focus on your task at hand for a series of quality pitches?"

"I'd like to think I can," he responded.

"So let's do that in your bullpen work. After you get warmed up, begin with your number one pitch and pitch five to ten quality pitches to a specific target. Now you don't have to use your catcher's glove. You can throw pitches to his knee guards, to his feet, and if you want to throw high, pitch to the top of his mask."

"I usually pitch to where the catcher holds his glove."

"Think about it, does he always put his glove to where you want to throw the pitch? In fact, sometimes is he late in getting his glove up?" I asked.

"It does happen," he responded.

"Jason, you don't want to be dependent upon your catcher. You are the king of the hill and you need to make the pitch through the specific target you wish. If your catcher is late in giving you a good target, use one of his knee guards and lock on to it just as if it was his glove."

Syd had Jason join me again for a couple days in the Orioles Fall Instructional League and again in the 2001 spring training.

Jason said to me after a bullpen session, "I like what I am learning from you, but sometimes I feel a little uneasy because I am not so conscious of what I am doing?"

I added, "Clearly to pitch unconsciously does not mean to pitch without consciousness. That would be quite difficult!"

I offered, "In fact when you were pitching 'out of your mind' you were likely more aware of your target. But you were not aware of giving yourself a lot of instructions, thinking about how to pitch the ball, how to correct past mistakes or how to repeat what you just did."

"Yeah, yeah, that's right. At Rochester, I think I was pitching out of my mind, but I was really focused on my target. And I didn't talk to myself very much," he stated and became rather animated.

I explained, "You were conscious, but not thinking, at least you were not thinking in words."

"Yeah, I wasn't talking to myself. It was so easy," he added.

I attempted to emphasize and clarify what he had done successfully, "When you were in this state you had an idea, you didn't have to 'try hard' to achieve the idea. It just seems to happen. And often you had great pitch command. You appeared to be immersed in a flow of action which requires your energy, yet resulted in greater power and accuracy."

"It sure did and I would really get on a hot streak for a while. My pitch command then was great," he said with a look of satisfaction.

I further commented, "The hot streak probably continued until you started thinking about it and tried to maintain it," I paused for Jason to think.

"Yes, and as soon as I attempted to exercise more control

over my pitching action, I lost it," he confirmed.

"Jason, you always have a choice. You can pitch one of two ways, either your attention focused inside your body or focused outside of your body. In forty years with some great pitchers, it is apparent to me that in game competition, the top pitchers ignore their body and are focused on things outside of their body." Then, I added, "Of course, it is your choice."

"This is making so much sense to me. Can you repeat that idea again so I can actually wrap my mind around it?" he asked.

"Yes, let me say it a different way. When you are focused inside your body, you are either highly aware of how a part or all of your body feels or highly aware of a thought. It is possible you could be highly aware of a series of thoughts, running through your mind."

I went on, "When you are focused externally, outside your body, your vision, your mind and your body are relegated to subconscious functioning. When you do that, there are few if any thoughts in your mind."

To get him thinking further about it, I asked, "What happens when someone asks you, 'What are you doing so differently that's making your fastball move so well today?' or 'What goes through your mind?"

"All kinds of thoughts," he said as he rolled his eyes.

"Once you begin thinking about how you are throwing, your streak will invariably end. You will lose your timing and fluidity as you try to repeat what you just thought you were doing."

"I want to pitch 'out of my mind!'," he said very firmly.

I took his lead, "You can learn to pitch 'out of your mind' on a regular basis. You can be unconsciously competent. You can learn to be so concentrated, so focused, that it seems that you are "unconscious" your mind will seem still as your body unconsciously functions at its peak, without interference from thoughts. "

I paused and then added, "This level of focus has no room

for thinking how well the body is doing, much less of the how-to of the doing. When you are in this state of concentration, you are really into the game and you discover your true capability."

He then asked, "But how do I do it without thinking? It seems like the last couple of years I have always been thinking about how to do something."

I attempted to clarify, "Most everything you physically do during the course of a day, your physical body's actions are controlled by your subconscious mind. You rarely think about what your fingers, hands, or feet are doing until you go on to the pitching field. Of course, off the field you can get by, even driving a car, without much conscious awareness of what you are doing."

I paused and before he could say anything I then added, "But the precision required in pitching performance, and the fact that most actions take place in less than one second, keep conscious performance from being very effective. Because you have pitched for so many years, your subconscious knows what to do. You just have to let it do its thing."

"Well, I am sure I am headed in the right direction," he said.

Jason was very effective in spring training. He earned a spot in the rotation out of spring training and has not relinquished it until late in the season. He was 3-2 in April then went 5-3 with an 8-5 record on July 1. On July 11, 2001, he has a winning record led the team in victories with eight and was among the league leaders in earned run average of 3.22. The Orioles were having another mediocre season, but Jason was a bright spot on the pitching staff.

I spoke to him at the All-Star break, and he told me, "Your training has made me much less stressed, more positive and visibly more confident as an athlete and as a person."

"It's a lot easier," the 6-foot-6 right-hander said. "Instead of worrying about 'I hope I do well,' it's more 'I wonder how good I'm going to do.'"

Syd Thrift told me, "It looks as if he is enjoying himself

on the mound this year, it's because he is. He credits his turnaround to a simple change in his mental approach."

Syd said he asked Jason, who said to him "I'm a lot more comfortable out there." He then added, "I've always had the stuff that I have right now. I had to get it under control mentally, and thanks to my work on my focusing process I think I have."

"I've come from a place where I was totally confused about what I was doing on the mound to being happy with not only my performance but myself," Johnson said. "There were times last year I wouldn't have thought that possible."

In retrospect, the prescription was simple. A better background of performance knowledge, an audio, and some eye charts were designed to help Johnson create a tunnel. By sharpening his focus, he could tune out crowd noise and other distractions, not even notice a hitter while fixating on the catcher's mitt. It is a talent usually taken for granted by those who watch the game but often difficult for those asked to perform while surrounded by 40,000 people.

"Your focus exercises helped me overcome my lack of concentration," Johnson said.

At the beginning of the three-week program, Johnson would hang one of his Vision Performance Cross Trainers on a wall. The drills had him pick out objects such as footballs and baseballs rather than numbers or letters. As the exercises became more demanding, Johnson would pick out a particular object in a prescribed order. Finally, he posted a second chart identical to the first. He would move his eyes from chart to chart, picking out objects at a quickening pace. To be successful, Johnson could not allow his gaze to wander.

He also worked on his focus control by using a 3D Depth Perception and Tracking Trainer. Initially, it was very difficult for him to use, but within time, he could do it easily.

"I found the focus card drills helped me clear my mind and get myself focused on my task at hand," Jason said.

"I think Jason deserves the credit for pursuing things in

every way to become a better player. He did a lot of things you don't have to do. And he's being rewarded," Thrift told the Baltimore press.

He then won two more games, before going on the disable list as he began suffering from severe fatigue. It turned out that he was suffering from previously undiagnosed diabetes.

Later in his career he was the first Major League Baseball player to get permission to wear an <u>insulin pump</u> on the field. He wore the pump on his belt on the left side of his lower back, to minimize the chance of it being hit by a bat or thrown ball.

Jason pitched in 11 seasons for the Orioles, the Tigers, and then had short stints with Cleveland, Boston, Cincinnati and the Los Angeles Dodgers.

Jason had a significant turnabout in his career. From time to time I have thought, "Would he been as great if he hadn't learned what we initially developed at the Kansas City Royals Baseball Academy and the concepts that were proven by Mark Littell, Paul Splittorff, and Greg Maddux?"

Perhaps Ewing Kauffman, Mark Littell, Steve Blass, Paul Splittorff, Greg Maddux and Syd Thrift were a big part of Jason's turnabout U-Turn.

Chapter 10

Pete Harnisch

A Phenomenal Career Turnabout

You will learn how a 7-year veteran pitcher sunk to the very bottom. His career appeared to be over and then he learned how to refocus and elevate his career. You will gain insights on how to master the ability to embed everything about your great pitches into your memory and discontinue implanting memories of poor pitches. You will also learn there is a readiness energy level for almost everything you do and that there is a flow of energy from the beginning of the action to the completion of the action. You will get in touch with when pitching effectively, you will find that there is a distinct flow of energy that takes place from the beginning to the completion of the action. Insights are offered on how to become a visual pitcher and not just a physical pitcher as you pitch while focused outside your body. As a visual pitcher, you will pay attention to things outside of yourself as opposed to being focused internally. This will allow you to ignore limiting feel oriented sensations of fatigue and discomfort as you pay attention to what you see. You will be in the here and now, and you will learn from your pitching experiences as you vividly see and recall pitches.

In mid-season 1997, the Reds were 43-56 under Manager Ray Knight. General Manager Jim Bowden appointed one of his scouts, Jack McKeon, to take over as manager. The Reds had a turnabout and went 33-30 the remainder of the season for a 76-86 season with a .475 ERA.

Jon Nunnally and Chris Stein had come over from the

Kansas City Royals and put a lot of spark in the team's lineup. But Jack and Bowden were not satisfied with their team's pitching. Jack and I had known each other for over twenty years, and he had seen firsthand the value of emphasis on the visual and mental side of the game with pitchers I previously worked with and that he managed.

In mid-February 1998 spring training, Jack asked me to talk with the pitching staff prior to its first 1998 workout. Jack, pitching Coach Don Gullet and I gathered with about 25 pitchers in the crowded media room at the Reds complex in Sarasota.

Jack said, "This guy helped a lot of my pitchers when I managed in Kansas City, Oakland, and San Diego. If you will not only listen but put some efforts it to using what he is going to tell you, you are going to become more productive. I saw the positive benefits to a lot of our pitchers with the Royals, A's and Padres."

The returning Reds pitchers from 1997 included Stan Belinda, Jeff Shaw, Dave Burba, Kent Mercker, Brett Tomko, John Smiley, Scott Sullivan, Pete Schourek, Jason Bere, Steve Cooke, Keith Glauber, Danny Graves, Pete Harnisch, John Hudek, Mark Kroon, Steve Parris, Mike Remlinger, Dennys Reyes, Jeff Shaw, Gabe White, David Weathers and Scott Williamson.

The leader of the 1997 staff was Jeff Shaw, who had 42 saves and pitched amazing for a losing team. The staff was 76-86 with a 4.41 ERA and Shaw had 42 of the 49 saves.

I emphasized to the pitching staff that when they had pitched well, there were some intangibles that they had used correctly, but when they struggled those intangibles had not been used effectively. We talked about such intangibles as target selection, energy control, fine and soft centering, visualizing pitches, visualizing their pitching actions and committing to a single task at hand. With such a large group, it was difficult for me to judge their response.

After the meeting, as I walked out to the field where the workouts were going to begin, suddenly a guy came up from behind. He put his hand on me and said rather animated, "We have to talk. I have had a lot of trouble with my focus. I think you can help me." I wasn't sure if he wasn't pulling my leg, but as looked him directly in the eye I could see his seriousness.

He went on to say, "I have had a horrible 4 years. In 1993, I was 16-9 for the Astros and everyone thought I was headed for an all-star career. Since then the harder I try, the worse I pitch. Can we sit down and go over a few things you discussed in the meeting?"

"Sure. Let me know when you are available."

The pitcher ran on to join his teammates in their pre-workout stretching program. I then realized that the pitcher was Pete Harnisch, a name I recognized because of the stories I had read about him when he was the New York Mets. Ironically, I didn't even know he was in the room.

Pete had a career year in 1993, but 1994-96 with the Astros and Mets and he was only 18-25 with an era over 4.00. Then he hit bottom in 1997 and was 2-4 for the Mets, Blue Jays and Brewers with an ERA over 7.00. The known to be typically upbeat Harnisch had endured a battle with clinical depression in 1997 reported to be due to insomnia issues and withdrawals from chewing tobacco.

I watched Pete throw in the bullpen. His pitches were all over the place. After a while, he became visibly upset. He was clearly a perfectionist, which I saw as a good thing. I could also see that he did not have any consistent approach. He rarely looked at his bullpen catcher. Perhaps he didn't need to. However, with the poor command I witnessed, I knew he needed to get better focused on the catcher's glove.

After practice, I sat down with him near his locker in the clubhouse.

"What you said this morning about concentration really struck a note with me," Pete repeated.

After some further chat, I reviewed in greater depth related ideas about soft centering and fine centering, centering internally within the body or externally on a specific target.

"Pete, when you have pitched at the top of your game like you did in 1993, what do you recall?" I asked.

"Frankly, I wasn't thinking about anything," he quickly responded.

"So you just trusted your ability?" I asked further.

"I sure did," he said as he nodded affirmatively.

"Well, it may take a little time but I am confident that you can get back to where you can trust your ability," I encouraged, knowing that he would likely doubt that bold statement.

"Pete, as a perfectionist, like most pitchers you probably analyze, replay and embed in your memory everything you did when you threw a bad pitch," I stated.

"You've got that right," he agreed.

"If you throw a great pitch, do you give it an equal opportunity? Do you analyze, replay and embed it in your memory to the degree you do when you throw a bad pitch?" I asked

"No, I can't say that I do," he looked directly at me and said.

"I encourage that you do just the opposite. You want to master the ability to embed everything about your great pitches into your memory and become ineffective at implanting memories of poor pitches," I paused.

I then added, "Another way of saying this is you are going to get where you want to be once you can capitalize on your successful pitches and learn to forget your poor pitches quickly."

He looked at me as if he thought I was full of it, "So, Doc, how in the heck do I stop, as you say, embedding poor pitches in my memory?"

"Pete, I am going to show you several ways, in which you can immediately clear your mind so that you are thinking of nothing. Additionally, I am going to show you how to occupy your mind with the proper thoughts. If your mind is occupied with the right thoughts, there is no room for the bad thoughts to enter your mind."

I proceeded to show Pete how he could use an eye switching technique to clear his mind and how to use visual thoughts to occupy his mind.

"Pete, when you want to clear your mind, simply find two targets. It makes no difference what they are, or how far away they are from you," I instructed.

As he looked around I said," It can be the toes of your two feet as you look down at the rubber it can be the two sides of the rubber you are standing upon, it can be the inner edge of each dugout, it can be the two sides of the batter's eye, whatever you choose is fine,"

I then added, "Simply start by looking at the one on your left and then switch to the right target and back. Repeat that full cycle at least three times."

I could see Pete doing it on the toes of his shoes.

When he finished, I said, "What are you think about now?"

"Nothing, absolutely nothing" he looked at me with a perplexed expression.

"How does that work?" he asked.

"Pete, it is really rather simple in that when you make quick, distinct eye movements you use a different part of the brain. By doing so, your attention leaves the area of the brain involved in thinking," I paused. "Quick eye movements give all of us an effective method for thought stoppage."

I also showed him how to focus on what he could currently see so that he was literally focused in the here and now.

"Well, that certainly is a new perspective for me. I kind of like it," he responded.

"Pete, let me caution you that in your desire to be perfect, you may have ten successes in a day and one failure, and as a perfectionist, you may pick upon on the failure to dominate your thoughts. The tendency may be to ignore what you do well and exaggerate what you do poorly. If so, you will lose perspective and drown yourself in guilt and remorse. Remorse is okay. But only if it leads to change."

"Well, I think you are absolutely right. But this is going to be a big change for me," he paused and looked at me again "But I believe i can do it if you will help me."

Another day in early spring training, I recall chatting with Pete at his locker after he had worked out in the weight room.

"Pete," he said, "what have you been centering upon in your bullpen workouts?"

"Truthfully," he replied, "I have been working on getting more velocity on my pitches. I feel like my command has been pretty good since I started narrowing my focus, but I just don't get enough velocity. Maybe I just don't have the arm strength I used to have."

"So let me ask you this, in the past have you ever felt like you were throwing the hell out of the ball, and expected your catcher after asking him something like 'how's my velocity?' to agree but he had a response that surprised you. For example, he might have said something like 'okay', and you were disappointed?"

"Yeah," he responded. "That used to happen all the time.

It always ticks me off. I look at the guy like 'do you know what you are talking about'?"

"Have you had other times when you thought you weren't throwing very fast, only to have your catcher tell you something like, 'Your fastball is great today. Let's keep firing it."

He quickly responded, "Yeah, that has happened too. It never made any sense to me, because it didn't seem to me I was throwing fast."

"Well, Pete, the difference probably was you were more centered on your glove when you were pitching with greater velocity. When you do that well, there will be less awareness of your body. You may feel like you are doing nothing. But it occurs when your focus is out over home plate and not within your body."

He thought and then responded, "I think you are right. When I try to throw hard, using your word I center in my body and it feels like I am trying like hell to throw hard. But when I get my attention out over home plate, it doesn't seem like I am putting as much effort into it."

He thought some more, "But I guess that's the feeling I want because it is always when my pitches apparently have more pop to them. It's like an out-of-the-body experience."

"The common factor in each of this description is what might be called 'mindless and or mindful' purposely using a couple of words for Pete that would get him thinking. "When you were mindless, your mind was rendered inoperative. When you were mindful you were likely thinking too much," I added.

"Now, that's what I need to do. I need to, what was that you said?" he asked.

He went on, "Oh I remember you said, 'my mind to be inoperative.' That is for me. I need to shut it down."

I said, "Pete another way to think about it is when you

are at your best you have 'thought stoppage.'"

"Yeah, yeah," he said, "That's exactly what I want. Thought stoppage is for me."

Watching Pete pitch in an inters-quad games it became apparent to me that he was a guy that would give more than 100 percent if he could. But I saw that great effort tensing him up at times, and could see how he often was losing his rhythm and timing.

A couple of days later after a game, Pete rushed up to me all excited, "That stuff is really working. It seems like I am hardly throwing, but my catchers tell me my velocity is great. Most importantly he said my fastball has great movement."

He then said, "I was felt great out there on the mound. I think I am on my way back! My demons are dying."

Pete was a clubhouse clown so that he may have been pulling my leg, but I could tell he was dead serious.

Pete thought for a minute, "The demons in my mind the last few years have been killing me. This is giving me a new way to attack and destroy them."

I observed, "The opponent inside your head is usually more formidable than the one you are facing. As a pitcher, you may realize that your greatest difficulty pitching quality pitch to your intended target is your thoughts making it harder to pitch than it really is."

"So instead of screaming at myself," he paused.

"Pete, if your mind is screaming, 'Pete you xxxx...' at any time thoughts like these are occupying your mind, your target will appear small and further away."

"Your right. Sometimes it has seemed that my catcher was a hundred feet away," he agreed.

"Your eyes lead your body and as boxing champion Muhammad Ali once said, 'I can't pitch to a target that my eyes can't see!' "

"That's great, did he really say that?" Pete asked.

"In truth," he said, 'Float like a butterfly; sting like a bee; your hands can't hit; what your eyes don't see!' Similarly, the eyes guide your body in your pitching actions."

"That's a good reminder. I want to pitch like Ali fought. He took it to his opponent," he said as he picked up on the analogy

"Pete, most all athletes tend to do too much talking to themselves, hoping to get their bodies to perform in the desired way. Ironically, your body does not understand English or any other spoken language. The real language of your body is visual information and visual pictures. Talking to yourself only works if it produces a visual image, which then communicates with your body."

"Ha Ha. I guess you are right. My body never reacted to me speaking to it in English, so I have usually cussed the hell out of myself," he laughed loudly

As we finished our talk, Pete was undressing and ready to go to the shower. So I gave him a quick summary thought, "When you have pitched your best, literally, you were visually conscious and unconscious mentally and physically. This is state of mind, a state of concentration, a state of awareness that you can have on a consistent basis from now on if you prioritize it as important."

"Well, I am certainly going to do that," he smiled.

Then with a serious look, he asked, "So how do I practice this?"

I advised, "In bullpen sessions, you will likely be focused inside your body a high percentage of the time. And that is fine for practice and preparation. But you need to finish each bullpen session when you pitch with your game face on. It is as if the white lines are painted, and the umpire has said 'Play Ball.' You imagine hitters in the box and you use your best pitching focusing loop."

I continued, "When the game starts, it becomes a different game. To perform at your peak, forget your body and focus on the outside on a specific target. It's time to become a visual pitcher. At game time, it's time to see your target just like a sniper and 'let it go.'"

"I'm going to do that," he said as he sounded committed.

My final emphasis was, "Pete, you are on your way to becoming a visual pitcher and not just a physical pitcher. When you are focused outside your body, you are a visual pitcher. Visual pitchers tend to be external, that is, they pay attention to things outside of themselves as opposed to being focused internally. As a visual pitcher, you will be able to ignore limiting feel oriented you will be in the here and now. You will be, therefore, less susceptible to stress than when you are an internal thought-oriented person. You will learn from your experiences because you will vividly see and recall your pitches."

"Wow, that is all good. You certainly have me thinking differently."

He paused and then added, "I think what you are describing is what I was doing in 1993 with Houston." And then he added, "But I didn't know what I was doing."

The 1998 staff had a few changes. Pete, Dave Burba, Mike Remlinger and David Weathers threw great in spring training. The Reds appeared to have a decent starting rotation and a great bullpen to start the season.

At the end of spring training, Jack McKeon said to me, "Some of these guys are beginning to get it. Burba is more focused than he was last season and Weathers looks like a different guy. And Harnisch has pitched really well the last couple of weeks. I really think he has a chance to turning his career around."

Pete started the second game of the season against the San Diego Padres. He gave up 4 hits and 5 unearned runs in 6 innings, but he only walked 2 which was a good sign.

A week later I saw pitch in San Diego. He pitched an 8 inning shutout, giving up only 4 hits and 2 walks. He left the game with a lead, but the Padres scored 3 in the bottom of 9th to win 302.

After the game, in the clubhouse as he was icing his shoulder he said to me, "Doc, I think I am getting this unconscious thing down. I like being unconsciously competent."

He followed it up on April 12 in Colorado and got his first victory with a 7 inning game in which he won 10-4.

Two weeks later, it became clear he had his game back. He beat the Phillies 1-0 with a 9 inning, 2 hit shutout. He was on his way. And the Reds were on their way back too.

At 31, Pete went 14-7 with a 3.14 ERA. It was quite a change. The prior season, 1997, in his first 10 games, he allowed 48 hits in 39 2/3 innings, walking 23 and striking out 22.

That same year, 30-year-old Steve Parris went 6-5 and Danny Graves was 2-1, had 8 saves and a 3.32 ERA. Gabe White though 5-5 had 9 saves and a 3.41 ERA.

In 1999, Pete opened the season and pitched will through August in September, he had severe shoulder problems but just kept pitching. Harnisch at 32 went 16-10 and led the Reds to a winning season. This was the best he had pitched since 1993 when he was 26.

In two seasons, he went 30-17 with a 3.19 ERA. This was a sharp contrast to his prior two seasons when he went 1-10 with a 5.95 ERA.

Pete led the 1999 Cincinnati Reds season to a spectacular season. They won 96 games in a 96-66 season though they lost 3 of their last 4 games. They ended up in a tie with the New York Mets. The 1999 National League wild-card tie-breaker game was a one-game extension to the regular season. It was played at Cinergy Field in Cincinnati, Ohio, on October 4, 1999. The Mets won the game 5–0, with starting pitcher Al Leiter pitching a two-hit shutout. As a result, the Mets qualified for the postseason and the Reds did not.

Though they lost, they truly had a great season. A 96-66 season following and 80-82 season in 1998 surprised baseball. Pete was the ace of the staff. He was a real warrior.

Unfortunately, his arm problems began in August 1999 and he was not his real self in September but he battled to the end. He did lose the last game of the season which resulted in the Reds needing a wildcard playoff victory.

At age 33 he entered the 2000 season with lingering arm difficulties. He pitched two more seasons but was 9-9 as his arm never fully recovered. He was just a shadow of his real self.

But in 1999, Pete led the Cincinnati Reds team to a great season. I am most certain that the baseball executives with the Houston Astros, New York Mets, Toronto Blue Jays, and Milwaukee Brewers could not believe what they were reading in the newspapers. And the owners of those teams no doubt wish they had had him back.

Pete had an amazing turnabout in his career. I have thought, "Would he been as great in 1999 if he hadn't learned what we initially developed at the Kansas City Royals Baseball Academy and the concepts that were proven by Mark Littell, Paul Splittorff, and Greg Maddux?"

Perhaps Ewing Kauffman, Mark Littell, Steve Blass, Paul Splittorff, Greg Maddux and Syd Thrift were a big part of Pete's late-career success.

SECTION II

THE PROVING GROUNDS

40 Years in a Laboratory

I believe when you do something hundreds times, and you get the same predictable results it is no longer anecdotal. It is common sense, and it is fact.

Laboratories prove concepts in experimental form and produce effective pharmaceutical drugs for treating numerous conditions. In this book, I am going to provide you insights that I proved in a unique laboratory that started developing in 1970 at the University of California at Davis. After forty plus years, it is now ready for more widespread use.

I never liked labs when I was in school as I found them boring. I certainly didn't want to spend the rest of my life as a laboratory technician. But I found a lab that really helped me tremendously.

The laboratories provided by sports performance allowed me to turn insights into some effective methods to be used by many. My laboratory was on the recreational or professional athletic playing fields, whether a court, a diamond, an arena, a course or a gym. For pitchers, the lab was the bullpen, the pitchers' mound, and the clubhouse.

This mobile laboratory allowed me to refine a variety of performance insights. I found these labs to be a great place where I observed pitchers getting in contact with themselves and becoming aware of many of their important performance strengths, weaknesses, and tendencies.

It was also a place where I observed how top performers learned to handle potential focus challenges and to focus on their task at hand. In a sports laboratory, when a person doesn't focus, they get immediate feedback. I believe the ideas that have been learned in the sports laboratory are relevant to almost any form of human performance including actions and occurrences in daily lives.

So sports provided me an idea ignition laboratory for human performance. In this laboratory, we focused on "how" recognizing that most people knew "what" they were supposed to do but didn't know "how" to do it. This search gave us more awareness of the role of one's senses, brain, and body in human performance. In my personal sports laboratory, I began to understand that in most performance actions the driving force behind the body is focus and very often it was a visual focus that was the real driver.

The laboratory of top human performance has been a great experience. And it continues to be a great experience ever day even forty plus years after starting with the Kansas City Royals.

Chapter 11

How I Learned

How2Focus

There were some key moments in my baseball career that shaped my understanding that I am sharing with you. I probably learned as much or more from my failures than I did from my successes. My working with MLB pitchers began the fall of 1972 with the Kansas City Royals Baseball Academy pitchers and the Royals Minor League Fall Instructional Pitchers. Mr. Ewing M. Kauffman, the original owner of the Royals, told me had very good feedback was favorably impressed with the work I did with his major league position players in 1972. He subsequently encouraged his new manager Jack McKeon to allow me to work with his pitching staff who then encouraged his pitching coach Galen Cisco to get on board. As a result, I had unusual freedom to work with all of the Royals pitchers. I've been working with MLB players over forty years and am now ready to share my insights on what works and what doesn't. Ryan has been working with me the last 15 and together we have refined our approach.

My convictions are strong on what I am sharing with you after forty years or working with youth, high school, college and professional pitchers. I have learned a lot from those that had great success, but I also learned a lot from those that unfortunately failed.

I have watched numerous pitchers who never took their potential in the bullpen to any consistent use in games.

Your managers and head coaches have watched you from

the viewpoint of your ability to pitch and win. Your pitching coaches and instructors have watched you carefully from the viewpoint of your pitching mechanics. We, on the other hand, have viewed pitchers from the viewpoint of their concentration, the use of their eyes and their consistency.

"Who are you?" you should be asking.

Whether you asked or not, I would like for you to know a bit about me. Very simply, I've had a passion for this game since I was three. I loved throwing and hitting a ball, any ball, large or small.

I pitched and learned a lot from my own mistakes. I certainly wish I would have known when I pitched what I began to understand in the early 1970's. Of course, it was too late for me at that time.

My early years in school were focused on being an athlete and getting good enough grades to get into college. But my real goal was to be a major league baseball player.

Some of my most memorable fun days as a child were listening to games on the radio and acting them out. I listened to so many Cleveland Indians games that it seemed as the players had become my friends. In reality, they were my virtual friends in the theater of my mind!

I experienced success and failure with each one of their efforts in the games I listened to. The Indians roster included some great players including Al Rosen, Roberto Avila, Luke Easter, Gene Woodling, Lou Boudreaux, George Strickland, Bob Feller, Bob Lemon, Mike Garcia, Herb Score, Mel Harder, Jim Hegan, Dale Mitchell, Larry Doby, Satchell Paige, Joe Gordon, Ray Boone, and Ken Keltner.

I vividly remember enacting out that I was pitching like Feller, Lemon, Garcia or Score as a Cleveland Indian beating the New York Yankees at Yankee Stadium.

From age nine to twelve, I had considerable success pitching and played with a lightweight, 10-inch rubber coated ball. I loved pitching the 10 inch because of it being lightweight the ball would dive in, out and down as if I was Yu Darvish. I'm glad we didn't have heavier, harder conventional baseballs.

I grew up in Alpaugh, California a hot central San Joaquin Valley farm town. Alpaugh, you may laugh at this, had 800 to 1000 residents when the migrant workers arrived to pick the cotton. Our K-8 school had a total of about 125 students. We played other elementary schools that were twenty to thirty miles away, and we usually won. All we did was play baseball. There wasn't much else to do in the hot and barren San Joaquin Valley farm towns.

My most fun was playing pickup games in a powdery dust field in the hot 100-110 degree days. At night, indoors we often hit ping pong balls with a rolled up magazine and had a terrific time. I further refined my eye-hand coordination hitting gravel pellets with a stick into an open field. I tossed my share of hard dirt clods at targets also. I know that when I played the game as a kid I could hit anything and everything, and I could throw accurately.

I matured physically rapidly, I was 5'11" and 185 lbs. in the eighth grade. My physical attributes made this game rather easy for me.

Alpaugh was too small to have a Little League team. Prior to the eighth grade, my family moved to Fresno, California and I became a Babe Ruth League All-Star.

I was a starting varsity player for four years at Bullard High School in Fresno and received All-League and All-City honors three of those years. I received four varsity baseball letters and a total of eleven varsity letters in three sports. I was the number one starting pitcher and when not pitching I played first base or in the outfield.

I had a phenomenal coach during my junior and senior year in High School. Coach Bob Bennett. Coach Bennett later won 1302 games as head coach at Fresno State University and was inducted into the Association of College Baseball Coaches Hall of Fame. I was really lucky to have Coach Bennett help me develop my baseball skills. He was my primary instructor of Pitching 101.

Later I was a starting pitcher and had the team leading batting average on a California State Championship Junior College team. At Fresno City College, I learned to love winning as I was a member of two state championship teams.

The following two years I pitched and eventually became the number one pitcher at the University of California at Berkeley, with a low ERA. My two-year ERA was 2.07, the 7th lowest in Cal Bear history, but my won-loss record was only 6-4. We didn't score many runs. At Cal, I learned to hate losing.

My head coach George Wolfman, just let us all pitch. But in my junior year former All-American pitcher John Rebelo returned and helped us develop a more professional-like approach. In those days, we were in the Pac 8 Conference and baseball in the Pac 8 was considered the premium conference in the United States.

I enjoyed a shutout victory over Stanford in 1964, the first shutout in the Cal-Stanford series that had started forty years earlier. A shutout was not pitched in that series for another thirty years. So I pitched the only shutout in 70 years of the series. When I was on I was pretty good. I just couldn't stay on as often as I wished.

Along the way, I played with future major leaguers Wade Blasingame, Andy Messersmith, Dick Selma, Mike Epstein, Rich Nye, Bill Frost, Dave Dowling and Larry Colton. In youth leagues, high school, and college I played against future major leaguers Tom Seaver, Jim Fregosi, Bob Garibaldi, Jim Lonborg, Pat Corrales, Darrell and Gary Sutherland, Randy Schwartz, Nelson Briles, John Boccabella and others.

I was proud. I thought I was headed to the show. My life's

goal was to be a major league pitcher. But I didn't make it. A shoulder injury at age 21, after 12 years of pitching, derailed my dreams. Surgeons weren't saving baseball players careers back in that day.

So I went on a search for a way to make a living. I decided to go back to the University of California at Berkeley become a Doctor of Optometry. And with that decision I had as a secondary goal that I was going to find out what made the difference between the famed Ted Williams, the last of the .400 Hitters and other players. Was it his outstanding eyesight, his extraordinary depth perception, or his phenomenal accurate and speed of recognition? I was going to find out as I studied optometry.

There were some key moments in my baseball career that shaped my understanding that I am going to share with you in this book. I probably learned as much or more from my failures than I did from my successes. My main talent was that I could paint the low outside corner with my slider and for whatever reason my fastball was difficult to hit hard. I did throw some no-hitters in high school and had a five for five day in a junior college game, so I know a little bit about success. Simply, I performed without conscious thought. On the other hand, I had some days I've tried to forget. I never could accept failing or losing.

Though I did reach my goal of becoming a major league player, in 1971, I pioneered some unique ideas into Major League Baseball. It led to a career of over 40 years working with top players in the game.

Little did I know that my career in professional baseball would not be as a player but would be as a consultant, a vision coach and that I would have the opportunity to work with many of the game's All-Stars as well as future Hall of Fame inductees.

I've been working with MLB players over forty years and am now ready to share my insights on what works and what doesn't.

My working with MLB pitchers began the fall of 1972 with the Kansas City Royals Baseball Academy pitchers and the Royals Minor League Fall Instructional Pitchers.

Mr. Ewing M. Kauffman, the original owner of the Royals, told me he had received very good feedback was favorably impressed with the work I did with his major league position players in 1972. He subsequently encouraged his new manager Jack McKeon to allow me to work with his pitching staff who then encouraged his pitching coach Galen Cisco to get on board. As a result, I had unusual freedom to work with all of the Royals pitchers.

Chapter 12

FALL INSTRUCTIONAL LEAGUE

How2Focus

Emphasis is made to not just work on the physical side of pitching, but to spend some time learning about the visual and mental sides of pitching. If you are struggling with some aspect of your pitching, this chapter will give you a new perspective that can help you achieve your goal. You will gain insights into how pitchers focus and how they think. You'll begin to understand why trying harder or blocking things out doesn't work. Benefits and negatives of different types of focus will be discussed. You will gain a perspective of how the proper feel is a byproduct of high quality, accurate visual thinking and not a byproduct of focusing within your body. You'll discover that when you control the visual side of the game, you also control the mental side of the game. But to do that you have to define your consistent task at hand. You'll also learn that if you don't know your task at hand and if you don't commit to it there is no way you are going to have the proper focus and concentration. You'll gain insights into an easily controllable process that places your attention on what you choose, so as a result you have the kind of concentration you need and want. You will learn that your eyes and your brain-based visual focus skills are the keys to the mental side of the game.

At the fall instructional league in 1972 Doctors, Bill Lee, Ray Reilly and I gave an introductory presentation to a group of pitchers. The group included the Instructional League pitchers of the Kansas City Royals minor leagues and Royals' unique Baseball Academy. The presentation was introductory about visual focus and concentration methods.

In the group were baseball executives and coaches included Syd Thrift, Buzzy Keller, Bill Fischer, Gary Blaylock, Bill Scripture, Chuck Stobbs, Steve Boros, Branch Rickey, Jr. and various staff people. As it turned out over time, these individuals were on their way to becoming very successful in their personal careers.

Among the many pitchers were Mark Littell, Dennis Leonard, Tom Bruno, Jerry Cram, Roy Branch, Gary Lance, Tom Linnert, Randy Hammon, and Hal Baird.

The Academy pitchers—including Tom Bruno, Gary Lance, Tom Linnert and Hal Baird—were passed over by all professional baseball scouts. In effect, they were told that they didn't have good enough arms to compete in professional baseball. In other words, these guys had no chance. They didn't know it, fortunately, but most of professional baseball's hierarchy was against them. They succeeded despite those invisible obstacles.

The minor league pitchers—Little, Leonard, Cram, Branch and Hammon—were drafted and had various level of expectations on having successful professional careers.

Bill Fischer, Chuck Stobbs, and Gary Blaylock were veteran pitchers and had coached several years. Fischer pitched 9 years in the major league baseball, between 1956 and 1964, and had a 45-58 won-loss record with a 4.34 era. Stobbs pitched 15 years in the major league baseball, between 1947 and 1961 and had a 107-130 era with a 4.29 era. Blaylock pitched 14 years in AAA ad 1 season in the major leagues in the minor leagues. He was 128-110 with a 3.72 era and in the majors was 6-4 with a 4.80 era. Stobbs the veteran was very open minded. Blaylock and Fischer were not.

Steve Boros was a former major league third baseman for

the Detroit Tigers. At the time, he was an A Ball Manager, but within a couple years, he was a major league coach. A few years later he was the manager of the Oakland Athletics and then the San Diego Padres. In addition to a great career as a player then a coach, then a manager and later a front office executive, Steve Boros was an exceptional human being. Steve was very open minded.

The meeting was at the end of a long and hot September day, and the pitchers were all tired. They were sitting back, slouched, with body language expressing, 'Why am I here?' 'This is a joke,' 'Are you kidding me, I have to listen to a couple of eye doctors?' 'What the heck does this have to do with me?'"

And likely they were thinking "Please let me out of here."

The minor league pitchers were all congregated in the back on the right side of the room, near the door, and the Baseball Academy pitchers all sat together in the front on the left side of the room.

Syd Thrift introduced me. Syd was a great orator and knew how to build someone or a topic up. He was already a believer in my training program's value because of what he had seen with the Major League position players.

Trying to motivate the pitchers, I recall his saying, "This is going to propel some of you to the major leagues. It depends upon you and how you put this valuable information to work." A couple of guys started to sit up as if they wanted to hear the message.

Others were probably thinking, "Here we go again. More bullshit."

To break the ice a bit, I told the pitchers that I pitched for eleven years through college, and I could relate to some of their challenges.

"Guys I am going to talk rather rapidly about several very important subjects. You don't need to take notes, just listen.

I will be around the next several days, so if you want to talk about anything in depth, I will be available to you," I paused.

I went on, "We are going to take a close look at focusing, concentration, and how you can best learn many aspects of your performance."

"Most of you guys went to school for quite a few years, am I correct?" They all nodded affirmatively. "Well in school you likely got graded on how well you thought in words. You were taught by teachers talking, and you had to repeat what they said on many of your tests."

They were all expressing agreement with what I said. One said, "I'm sure glad I am out of school."

"In baseball word thinking only goes so far. You have to learn how to think in pictures. I will refer to it as visual thinking, picturing, imaging or visualization. I also want you to remember in pictures in what we can call visual memory as opposed to verbal memory."

Chuck Stobbs spoke up, "This is kind of interesting to me. When I pitched, I don't remember using words very much. I really didn't think too much when I was on the mound."

Coach Bill Fischer added, "For me it was all about finding the right feel."

I looked at the pitchers in the room and said, "Feel thinking is what you do, but you can get better if your actions are preceded by visual thinking. In fact, visual thinking produces that feel. You are going to learn that visual thinking will help you gain the feel you need to execute many of your actions."

"How many of you struggle with getting the right feel for your various pitches?" Almost every pitcher in the room raised their hand.

I then asked the group several other questions. I asked the group, "How important the physical side of pitching?" That was an easy question for them to respond, and they responded in full agreement.

"It's everything," one replied and the others nodded affirmatively.

I then asked, "Since the physical is so important to pitching, how much of your time are you spending on training and developing the physical side of your game?"

Another pitcher said, "100%. All the time." And again I had a room of nodding heads.

"So if that is the case, how important is the mental side of the game?" I asked.

There wasn't a quick response and I noticed the pitchers looking at one another, likely waiting for someone to respond.

"It's just as important as the physical," said Hal Baird. Baird was a young Academy pitcher who after his professional career became a long-time successful head coach of the Auburn University Tigers baseball team. Hal became a very good AAA pitcher.

"So if the mental side of the game is as important as the physical side of the game, do you spend as much time training and developing the mental side of your game," I asked in general.

Again there was silence. None of the pitchers had a response.

I observed, "Okay, I get it. The mental side is very important to you, but you don't know how to train and develop it. You just have it or you don't."

"As far as having a good mental side of the game, it comes and goes," said Gary Lance another Academy pitcher who within time would pitch at the AAA level.

Without responding, I changed direction and asked, "Well, tell me this. If the physical side of the game and the mental side of the game are each like 50% importance for a total of 100% of what is important, how important is the visual side of the game."

I asked. I also knew I had these guys stumped. They looked around but didn't respond.

I went on, "Perhaps you don't think it is important but can you pitch while wearing a blindfold?"

The group chuckled.

I quickly said, "Without your eyes you can't see your target, your balance will be very shaky. Once you throw the pitch you will have no idea if you hit your target or which manner you missed it. You also wouldn't see the hitters' reactions to your pitch." I paused and then added, "Oh yes, you wouldn't know what sign you were given."

I went on "How effective can you pitch, play defense, hit or run the bases if you were a blindfold?" They all laughed more and looked at one another. I knew they were likely thinking "This guy is a little weird."

I then asked, "How good is your focus if you wear a blindfold?"

I quickly added, "How confident are you if you wear a blindfold?"

I then asked, "How good is your coordination if you wear a blindfold? Would you have good mechanics if you wore a blindfold?"

"Without your answering, I want you to consider that everything you do as a pitcher begins with how and what you visually focus open and ends with what you visually focused upon. Your use of your eyes is vital."

After a pause I added, "You could never picture anything if you hadn't first seen it with your eyes."

"I think you will agree that the visual side of the game is a factor as well. However, isn't it difficult to know just what that the visual side is in pitching?"

Hal Baird said, "Isn't the mental side of the game 90% visual?"

I then recalled that Hal was one of the Academy pitchers that I had given an introductory presentation during the spring. He was already familiar with the visual approach to pitching and had seen some success.

"Hal, you are correct. In my experience when you control the visual side of the game you also help the mental side of the game," I responded.

Hal said, "Doc, I think most of us recognize that the mental side of the game is really important to us. But we don't know how to practice it."

"I understand. So let's talk about a part of the mental side of the game that you each can practice and gain a better ability to do properly."

I went on, "How many of you have been told you need to focus better, that you need to concentrate?"

They started moving in their seats nodding in agreement. Of course, no one wanted to speak up.

I looked over at Buzzy Keller, and he said, "I've been telling everyone of you Academy pitchers that you have to learn how to concentrate better. I see concentration breakdowns all the time. And once you guys lose it, you never seem to get it back."

Minor League Manager Steve Boros added, "The same applies to you minor league pitchers. The reports from all your coaches indicate you lack concentration."

I followed up and said, "So guys, if you were my coach and told me that I needed to concentrate, let's suppose I said, 'Sure, but coach how do I concentrate?' What would you tell me to do to concentrate better?"

After some delay the minor league pitching coordinator Bill Fischer, a former major league pitcher said, "Try harder."

"Okay," I paused, "Isn't that like bearing down?"

He said, "Damn right, these guys need to bear down."

I paused and let them think about what Coach Fischer said and then said, "So what happens when you try harder or bear down?"

I could see that there was a little conflict arising in most everyone's mind. The idea of bearing down was a good one and a very common baseball expression.

I then said, "Don't you tend to tighten up. Doesn't tension set in and result in you losing your rhythm? When you try too hard, even your mind can begin to race?"

Most of the pitchers nodded. Dennis Leonard said, "I have to relax my body to pitch. I've tried to try harder, and it just doesn't work for me."

Leonard began a 12-year career pitching very successfully in the major leagues just a couple of years later. Only four years later, in 1976, he was pitching for the Royals in the American League Championships against the New York Yankees.

"Maybe there is a better approach. What is another thing you tell me to do to concentrate?" I asked.

"Block things out!" said one young, strong-looking young man with a southern drawl, Mark Littell.

I nodded "It is true that when you have the best concentration you aren't aware of anything else. However, let's try something. At this moment block out the way your body feels. Block out any fatigue or sleepiness. Block out any background sounds. Block out any thoughts about yellow grizzly bears." I then paused. Everyone laughed thinking about those yellow grizzly bears.

"Did you notice in your effort block everything out you became more aware of them?" I asked. Everyone nodded and gently shook their head in agreement

I went on, "Blocking out how your body feels, your fatigue, any background sounds, and those yellow grizzly bears just makes you more aware of them. Blocking out simply does not work."

They all seemed to agree as they looked around at one another.

A hand flew up. It was Roy Branch the Royals number one draftee. He said, "Hey, Doc, I think concentration is about desiring something. You have to want it."

I responded, "That is true, some people think that concentration is just a matter of wanting something enough. They think it is about desire. Do you think that when you haven't concentrated on the mound, you had a lack of desire?"

Branch thought and then said, "Well, not really." He thought for a moment and then said, "I think it is because I desire too highly to pitch well. I get too amped up. I guess I try too hard."

Branch later had a cup of coffee pitching in the Major Leagues and pitched a total of 9 seasons in the minor leagues.

Syd Thrift stood up and said, "Fellows, it is very clear to me that none of you have a good idea on how to concentrate. I think this is relevant to each of you."

I went on, "When you don't pitch well what are some of your questions you ask yourself?"

No one offered anything, so I said, "I suspect they are something like the following," 'What's wrong with me?' 'Why isn't my breaking pitch so inconsistent?' 'Do I need to throw harder?' 'Am I pushing off enough or falling off properly?' 'Am I extending or am I following through?' And so on."

I paused and then went on "You need to ask yourself, questions help you? The right questions can be helpful. Do some of your questions just create a lot of noise and no answers?"

The pitchers were starting to look more interested in what I had to say.

Changing directions, I said, "You guys have a lot of different circumstances that occur in a game. Whether you are starter pitching 100 or more pitches per game or a reliever for an inning or two who is going to deliver 15-20 bullets, in every situation you have a task at hand. In fact, no matter what the score may be, losing or winning, instructional league, intrasquad game or an in-season game you have the same task at hand. In fact, if you were to move from A Ball, through AA, on to AAA and into the major leagues, you still have the same task at hand."

I looked around the room and asked, "What is your task at hand?"

I pointed at the sleepiest looking guy in the room, who responded and everyone laughed, "Uh, I don't know."

Then a pitcher put his arm up and said, "Throw strikes."

I pointed at another who said, "Get guys out."

Another added, "Stop them from getting runs."

And another one said, "Win."

Still another said, "Execute my mechanics."

I then tried to wake them all up with a strong, "You guys are all wrong."

I paused so they would think and then said "You guys are here trying to pitch as a professional, and you don't even know the common task you have."

I realized I was likely getting under their skin by challenging them in that manner. To lighten up the atmosphere, I said, "Guys those are great goals. They are each correct. But goals are great if you achieve them. You'll feel good. But if you don't achieve your goals, you can go into a downspin."

I amplified the thought, "Chasing goals leads to a roller coaster ride. You feel up when you get it done and plunge downward when you don't achieve your goals. It can be a terrifying ride."

As they were no doubt thinking about their ups and downs, I added, "I want you to consider a different approach. Your goals are excellent, but the way you reach your goals is to commit to a very specific and consistent task at hand."

I let them think further and then suggested "I suggest you say something to the effect of 'My task at hand is to pitch a quality pitch through a specific target.'"

I could see them nodding positively and then added, "If you don't know your task at hand and if you don't commit to it there is no way you are going to have the proper focus and concentration."

Coach Stobbs said, "What you are saying is at the heart of the ideas of pitching one pitch at a time." He looked around and even Blayock and Fischer were nodding.

I then added, "We are talking about every pitch, no matter what the game's situation is at the time. We are talking something you can control. If you would commit to throwing a quality pitch to a specific target on every pitch how effective would you be?"

Dennis Leonard offered, "I would be lights out." As of the next season, 1973, Leonard was "lights out."

I looked at Dennis and asked, "Have you ever pitched a quality pitch through a specific target." He thought about it and nodded affirmatively and confidently.

I said, "Each of you have, and when you have done it you have pretty effective. Sometimes the luck of the hitter has resulted in something other than intended, but you did the right thing in pitching a quality pitch through your specific target."

I could see the pitching coaches Fischer, Blaylock and Stobbs nodding in agreement.

I continued, "There will be times when things don't work out as intended, you must ask yourself, 'Did I make the right decision in selecting the type of quality pitch and selecting of your intended target.' This is a learning experience and with experience, your decisions will get better and better."

Syd Thrift spoke up, "Did you fellas hear Dr. Harrison says 'pitch a quality pitch?' He didn't say 'Throw a quality pitch?' He also said 'Through your intended target' and not 'to your intended target.' Do you understand why he has chosen those words?"

Tom Linnert, an Academy pitcher who later pitched in AAA, spoke up, "I have always thought of throwing to a target. I don't do it very well. I think the idea of pitching through my target makes a lot of sense to me."

Syd, who was a former left-handed pitcher himself in the Yankees organization prior to injuring his arm, looked at the Academy pitchers and said, "This is going to become your mantra."

Linnert said, "I like the idea of 'Through the target.' Thinking about it gives me a good feeling."

I said, "So you guys don't seem to know how to help me how to focus. I suspect you have the same difficulty helping yourself focus."

They almost all nodded affirmatively.

"I think we can all agree that focus is a very important part of pitching. In fact, if you are going to be able to pitch effectively as you move up the ladder of minor league baseball, to the major leagues, focus is going to be one of your most important attributes."

"It sure is," responded Hal Baird.

"As important as it is, so far you fellows have not really know what your task at hand is to be and you don't know how to explain to someone else how to focus?" I asked.

I looked at the Baseball Academy pitching coordinator, veteran Major League pitcher and Academy Pitching Coach Chuck Stobbs, who offered, "They must learn to focus. Without high-quality focus, their pitching mechanics will regularly deteriorate no matter how hard they work on their mechanics. A loss of focus may very well end up in your having a sore arm and be unable to pitch."

I looked at Chuck, "That is amazing to hear that from you." Everyone knew that Chuck began pitching in the major leagues at age 17 and stayed for 15 years.

"Your pitching mechanics are going to breakdown if you aren't focused correctly," I exclaimed. "Your focus is vital."

Steve Boros spoke up, "Every single one of you in this room struggle with your pitching mechanics, so listen up, this is very important."

On a roll, I turned to the pitchers, "I want to introduce to you a new word. It will seem a little strange until I help you understand it. The word is 'centering'. Everyone centers their attention one hundred percent of the time. When your centering is solely on your task at hand, you are focused and the proper concentration. Anytime you are centered on something other than your task at hand, you don't have good focus or concentration."

Mark Littell spoke up, "Doc," he paused as if he was afraid to ask the question, "What in the world do you mean by using the word centering?"

"Great question, young man," I replied. "I am not referring to the middle of something. And I am not referring to getting yourself lined up. In fact, I am not referring to meditating or doing yoga or something like that." Then I paused so they could all keep thinking and hopefully ready for my answer.

I then elaborated, "Centering is an active effort of directing your energy to a target to process relevant, available information. It isn't about aiming your eyes. It isn't about blocking things out. Centering is about actively processing the available and pertinent information radiating from the target that is part of your task at hand. It's a proactive action that you can direct and control."

I took a breather so they could think about it and then added, "Centering produces a focused feeling like all of your energy is directed toward your intended target."

"It sounds like centering is what occurs when I get locked in," said Hal Baird.

"Yes, Hal." Then I added, "Guys have you ever pitched a pitch while focused on something small within your catcher's glove?"

Several responded "Yes."

When you focus on a small target, we would like for you to think of that as a fine center. A fine center is full attention to a very small target or area. It might be the dark pocket of your catcher's glove, an edge of the catcher's glove, or even a scratch or crevice on his knee guard. It's a little bit of an out-of-body experience."

"At other times you may be aiming your eyes toward your catcher, but seeing or being aware of a much wider area." I paused, "When you see a large area that should be thought of as a soft center."

Dr. Bill Lee said, "I had always, of course, been aware of the importance of focus. It was not until Dr. Harrison, and I experimented with drills with local college pitchers, however, that I realized the importance of visual focusing in controlling body and muscular movement. The most important thing is it is trainable and approvable."

Dr. Reilly, the human factors psychologist, added his

thoughts, "I have already observed the positive impact that this training provides. I believe this training eliminates performance anxiety by releasing the conscious thought and reducing inner chatter."

Syd Thrift jumped up, "That's just what we need."

I then offered, "Our approach involves training the eyes to access the visual centers in the brain to increase the speed the body reacts or acts. We believe eye-mind-body control is the essence of athletic greatness."

"We know that pitching is looked at from a very physical point of view. We also know that the mental side of the game is considered an important component," I paused for a moment.

"But we are going to show you how something you likely have never thought about, and that is that the visual side of the game and the use of your eyes has a big impact on the mental and physical sides of the game." I stopped to let them think about what I said because I knew it was to be a very strange thought to both the pitchers and the coaches.

Ray Reilly the Kansas City Royals psychologist who all the coaches knew spoke up and said, "Guys, I have to tell you initially I thought this was going to be the goofiest thing in the world. I was very resistant. I went to California to meet with these guys only because Mr. Kauffman ordered me to. After seeing them work with players, I became convinced they have something truly unique that will help us develop our players."

I added, "It's about improving your performance by utilizing pictures your actions, locking in your attention and using your eyes appropriately."

Again I looked at Stobbs and asked him, "Coach when you pitched did you 'picture' the pitch before you pitched it?"

Chuck thought for some time and then said, "I have never

thought about it, but I believe I did. When I pitched well, I could see the trajectory and the spin of my pitch going to my target. So I guess I did."

I then asked Chuck to "picture" his some of his most successful pitching outings. In asking Chuck, I expected other coaches in the room would all be relaying some of their more successful outings.

"Doc," he replied, "it's a lot easier for me to picture my lousy outing." Everyone laughed.

"Chuck, we think your pitchers should learn it is important to picture what they want and not picture what they want to avoid."

"Why does picturing work so well?" he asked.

"When you picture what you want to occur in any situation, you will know in advance what to pay attention to and how to react. You use the same pathways in your brain that will be used in your actions. You, in effect, wake up your brain and prepare it for success," I responded.

"But can't you perform without picturing?" Chuck countered.

"Sure you can, but when you don't, you're forced just to react. Everything that will come to mind will be unplanned and most likely inaccurate. Reactive performance sometimes is superb, but too often it can be quite poor."

Bill Lee said, "We will be encouraging your players to picture actions and talk to themselves less. We are also going to train them 'how' to focus."

He carried on, "Ironically, when they talk to themselves their body does not understand words. Telling themselves to take a step or a swing will not make their body do it. Muscles do not hear!" added Bill Lee. "We all tend to use a lot of words. The words must create a detailed, accurate picture to be effective."

Bill looked at me and said, "I think they need a better understanding of centering."

I took Bill's cue and slowly said, "It is important that see centering as an active effort of directing your energy to a target to process relevant, available information. It isn't about aiming your eyes. It isn't about blocking things out. Centering is about actively processing the available and pertinent information radiating from the target that is part of your task at hand. It's a proactive action that you can direct and control. An active centering effort produces a focused feeling."

I then added, "It is a process of attending to all of the available information that comes from what you are centering your attention on. It is the active process of directing all of your energy through the one appropriate sensory system on the specific task at hand. Since it is physical, 'centering'—unlike 'concentration'-it is a process each of you are capable of controlling and learning."

I let them think about it for a full minute or so.

I then added, "Remember, centering produces a centered feeling like all of your energy is directed toward your intended target. It's a feeling of total control. It's a feeling of being 'locked in'."

Wanting to give them a good analogy I added, "For example, a baby who sees a milk bottle, starts moving and perhaps crying until it gets the bottle, and obviously enjoys savoring every morsel as he or she grips the bottle tightly with their two little hands. This is a great example of centering their focus via a sensory system on a primary information source—the bottle. The baby used its sensory system of vision, taste and touch to really get into that bottle."

"Another way to think about your visual centering is to comparison yourself with a flashlight. You can be like a flashlight with a very wide, not very bring beam or you can place a shield over your flashlight with only a small pinhole. The light that comes out of the pinhole will be narrow, but will project further because it is very bright. In a dark room, the wide flashlight allows for a soft center. The pinhole flashlight allows for you to only fine center your attention."

I continued, "With a laser-like centering there is a unique sense of your energy going directly to a target. It is as if you are going to attack the ball, the glove, the net or the opening, in fact, it as if you are going through the ball, glove or net."

I let them think and then added another thought, "A fine or soft visual or auditory centering is an external focus. A fine or soft physical centering or centering on thoughts is an internal focus."

Buzzy Keller said, "Bill your demonstrations and analogies are great. Do you have any other you can think of that can help these guys get a firm grasp on centering?"

I responded, "Sure, Buzzy, a simple demonstration will likely help you understand the active process required to have high-quality focus. Look at one of the light switches in this room. You were likely able to do that easily and a quick, glimpse was sufficient."

"As you are now looking away from the switch, was the switch up or down? What is the length, width of the switch? What color is the plastic plate surrounding the switch?"

"Now that you had to process more information than was required in the quick, shallow focus did you find yourself more tuned in seeing the light switch? The processing of information is the differentiating factor. You can center within all of your senses, including what does your shoe feel like in the area of your right toe? What variety of background sounds can you hear? Are the background sounds rhythmic, loud, and changing in terms of inflection? Listening for the just noticeable differences requires the processing of available information and is the key to proactive centering."

Syd looked at the side of the room with the Academy pitchers and said, "I think you guys too often are in a soft center when you pitch."

I had such good attention in the room I decided to give them another demonstration of the concept of centering, I asked that they look in the middle of the chalkboard at an "x" I had written on the board. I then asked them to think about their bodies. "Think of the heel of your right foot. Now think of the fingers with which you grip a ball." I noticed some had stopped looking at the "x" on the chalkboard. I reminded them to keep looking at the "x".

I then asked for them to think about some of their best pitching performance of the season and followed that by asking that they think about some of their worst pitching performances. Several of the pitchers closed their eyes, some looked up and away from the "x" and a couple had some very slow eye blinks.

I then asked that they listen to all the background sounds in the building. At about that time, a door closed down the hallway. There was also a sound of a radio in an adjoining office. I shuffled my feet.

"So guys, I want you to think about how focused you stayed on the "x" on the board. You started with a fine center, but you naturally went into a soft center. At times you blinked, closed your eyes, or looked away. But even when you aimed your eyes at the "x" you did not actually see it. You were rather glazed and when you were aware of seeing you saw the entire front of the room."

Most everyone nodded.

"So how well have you pitched when you were in a soft center?" I asked.

Tom Bruno offered, "I am all over the place. I have no control of my pitches." Bruno was a big 6 foot 6-inch-tall

Baseball Academy pitcher who was pitching in the major leagues four years later.

I responded, "A soft center visually has its benefits. For one, you could sense that you are more relaxed because you aren't trying to direct your attention. But it is a general focus, and you tend to get general results."

"So you guys need to some experimenting. I'm not telling you what you should do. You simply have to find out whether you are at your best when you are soft centered or when you are fine centered. We are going to meet again two days from now and by then hopefully most of you will have · pitched in a game in the bullpen and should be able to give me some good feedback."

Syd stood up and said, "Fellows, you are learning more about the mental side of the game than likely any other pitcher has ever heard. No one else has been exposed to this. Fortunately, our owner, Mr. Kauffman could see the benefit and has provided these fellows to help us. The physical side of pitching will always be critical. You have to have the ability. But you guys are at the stage in your young career that the mental side of the game is what is going to make a difference. And isn't it amazing that your eyes and your brain-based visual focus skills are the keys to the mental side of the game. Amazing stuff!"

Everyone was tired, and we called it a night.

Chapter 13

EARLY SPRING TRAINING
How To Pitch Lights Out

The experiences of other pitchers and their challenges of being consistent will offer insights and solutions. You will gain insights on why you can pitch great and then all of a sudden lose it. You'll also learn how your bullpen sessions and you're own the mound performance can be different. You'll also learn some insights on why as a starting pitcher you may struggle in your first inning. Common challenges in learning are highlighted. You are going to learn about the four stages of learning to reflect key ingredients for mastering just about any skill you can dream up. With these insights, you can proceed to the highly focused, highly capable stage of 'unconscious competence where you don't even think about what you are doing.

The next February, in early spring training, only the pitchers and catchers were in camp for the first week. One evening we had a team pitchers meeting after dinner. It had been long, hot day, but the pitchers seemed to be very attentive.

I recognize many of the pitchers that I had worked with at Fall Instructional League.

I opened up with "This young man," I pointed at Dennis Leonard, "said last fall that if he did what we were talking about he would pitch 'lights out.' I happen to think you all can, so tonight let's go over some things that should help you 'pitch lights out.'"

I looked at the group of pitchers and said, "Before we get into the main things I want to go over tonight, did any of the ideas we worked on at Fall Instructional League made any sense to you so far?"

Most heads nodded up and down. Of course, the pitchers that didn't pitch in Instructional League had no idea what I was talking about.

"As a review, last fall we made and emphasis on your learning to personally control your capability of centering. We talked about a 'soft center' which is what you normally do so that you take in a wide picture. And we also talked about having a 'fine center' in which your focus is pinpointed.

Sensing that I had some agreement, I then said, "In the past you likely pitched in the bullpen in a soft center. In effect, you are training and developing your ability to easily soft center. You are so good at it that it has become a natural reflex. Soft centering is too easy for you."

A big, older looking minor league pitcher raised his hand, "I think this centering idea relates to why sometimes I pitch great for a few innings and then totally lose it." Later I learned this pitcher to be Randy Hammon, who later pitched in AAA.

Randy continued, "I can think back to times that I was riveted, as you say 'fine centered' on the catcher's glove and sailing along. And then for some reason I would start pitching with no awareness of the catcher, at best I had some form of 'soft center'. When that happened, I lost command, got behind on hitters and they would rock me. "

Looking around the room, I could see that many of the minor league pitchers could relate to what Randy was saying.

He went on to say, "I now realized I would start thinking, perhaps after a bad umpires' call on a pitch, and then I would go into a soft center and stay there on most pitches."

I went on, "Whenever you are thinking about anything, good or bad, you are in a soft visual center." I paused.

I then emphasized, "When you work on mechanics or get involved in thought, even if positive thoughts, you are in a soft visual center."

Tom Linnert, a Baseball Academy pitcher, said, "This idea of soft centering and fine centering helps me understand why sometimes I have a lousy bullpen session and then get into the game and pitch effectively. I think when I get on the mound in a game, I actually get better focused."

Linnert a small 165 lb. Left-Hander ended up pitching at the AAA level.

"So should I forget wanting to get better mentally?" asked Roy Branch, the number one draft choice asked.

"Not exactly. You will get better mentally if you take the proper approach. But just like physical mechanics, if you focus on the wrong approach you can get worse."

I could see a couple of the pitchers thinking about that one.

I went on to say "Do you guys know that when you pitch without a pinpoint focus, you are practicing, training and developing the ability to soft center. This is what commonly happens when you go to the bullpen and work on your mechanics?"

I knew I shocked them with this idea. Risking full rejection, because it was so counter to the norm, I quickly clarified.

"In the bullpen, there is a time you should just be focusing on mechanics, but you also need to work on the rhythm and tempo you will use in a game, focus the same way you will do in a game."

A young Baseball Academy pitcher offered, "I have often

wondered why I often can't get past the first inning. And if I do, I pitch much better. I think a lot of times in my first inning my thoughts are all over the place. I'm usually worrying about my mechanics. If I can make it through first inning a lot of time, I sort of settle down and then I do as you say I 'fine center' on the glove."

Coach Bill Fischer spoke up, "Are you telling these guys to not work on their mechanics?"

"No. I am not saying that coach," I responded.

And then I added as I looked directly to various pitchers and not Coach Fischer, "When you center your attention within your body, feeling a part of your pitching mechanics, you go to a soft visual center."

I added, "It may be okay. Just be aware of what you are doing. It is the right thing to do. You must work on your mechanics. Coach Fisher and the other coaches will tell you what they want you to work on and you need to do it. But just understand that it puts you in a soft visual center," I paused.

I then said, "You should now be thinking, so what?"

"Here's the so what. Look at that 'x' on the chalkboard and think about how big it appears. How clear are the chalk marks? Notice how the two lines that make the 'x' are not equal lengths, nor are they equal widths. There is a very slight difference in each line."

I could tell they were rather puzzled.

"Notice that when you looked at the 'x' with such intent to see the details, you were not aware of your body, you were not thinking and you had such a narrow visual focus, you were not aware of anything else. This is what we call a fine visual center."

I paused so they could think about what I just said, "Your attention is on a very small area, and you were not aware of anything else. That's when you are fine centering. Does that make sense?" They were nodding.

Buzzy Keller looked at the Academy pitchers and said, "This makes a lot of sense to me."

Keller looked at the pitchers and said, "You guys have to understand that there is a lot to learn. And if you are going to learn you need to learn something about how to learn."

Buzzy and Chuck's comments prompted me to think about failure and the early stages of learning so I offered, "You were all an infant once and when you were you were pretty adept at learning. As an infant, you were willing to fail, but often didn't give up until you got what you wanted."

"Yes, your actions were usually stimulated by desire, or at least by interest. That desire frequently was associated with the desire to touch, to taste or see better."

I could see they were thinking a bit and I added, "We were all an infant once. Though we likely can't remember what we did check infants out." I watched the pitchers looking at each other as if they are thinking "Where is this guy going?"

I continued "When infants start attempting to set up. They don't quit if they fall over, they do accept a helping hand, and then continue striving set up until fatigue sets in. Once fatigue does set in, infants seize the opportunity to lie down and relax. The same quest for success follows with crawling, climbing up and walking."

Steve Boros summarized my thought by saying, "Infants, as they become toddlers, enjoy the success of achieving their intended mission. They get frustrated and cry about it, but keep on moving toward their goal. At least, that's been the case with my kids."

After a pause Steve then said, "There is a lot of great information here. But how do these guys learn how to use it?"

It was as if Steve had set me up for the next topic I wanted to cover.

I said, "I want to introduce you guys to an idea that began a few years ago by a man named Noel Burch, an employee of the famous business relations company, Gordon Training International."

I was sure they were wondering what this had to do with pitching.

I went on to say, "While Burch himself was no scientist, famed psychologist Abraham Maslow found Burch's ideas of four stages of learning to reflect key ingredients for mastering just about any skill you can dream up."

I could see some of the players rolling their eyes as if "What in the heck does this have to do with pitching?"

I went on "Not having a skill or not have learned how to do something is similar to when a baby that it does not know how to tie shoe strings. That baby has zero frustration and can be blissful. It is the common stage of blissful ignorance before learning begins. This stage is like not knowing how to drive a car, ride a bike, throw a ball or swing a bat yet not having any concern that your technique is not correct. Burch labeled this happy yet incapable stage as 'unconscious incompetence.'"

I could see several of the players smile a little bit because I am sure they could relate to being 'unconsciously incompetent.'"

"Likely at this stage, one's focus or centering is all over the place. There is not consistent focus progression or loop." I said that setting them up for a better understanding later.

I then added, "But then the baby sees that others can tie a shoe string and thinks, 'I don't know how to do that.' Similar to the baby this is the stage of not knowing how to drive a car, ride a bike, throw a ball or swing a bat and getting frustrated and determined. You notice that others can drive a car, ride a bike, throw a ball or swing a bat properly. "I know that I don't know how to do this, yet."

"This is the most difficult stage, where learning begins, but usually you experience a lot of upset. Maslow labeled this awareness yet incapable stage as 'unconscious incompetence.'"

I could see the players, and the coaches, looking more interested. "Unconscious incompetence occurs when focus or centering is internal on thoughts or feeling parts of the body." I was again setting the up for later understanding."

"So the baby looks at his shoes and gets his hands on his lace up shoes and consciously begins to tie his shoes. You might finally get in a car, on your bike, with a ball in your hand or a bat in your hands decide you are going to 'Just do it.' The baby and you are very determined you are going to try extra hard to get your goal accomplished. It is a very self-conscious and awkward stage as you and the baby are very aware of every next move you are going to make. You are very conscious of what you are doing. Often the timing is off and the coordination of the body's actions is less than perfect. At this stage, you may feel somewhat better, but still not be very smooth or fluid in doing your desired actions. There is often a feeling of awkwardness as you need to continually think carefully about what you are going to do next. And, even when your actions are done correctly because you are so conscious of your body you likely don't do the action as fast as is desired. Maslow labeled this somewhat capable stage as 'conscious competence.'"

"Conscious competence occurs typically when focused internally, to some degree, but not as intently as in unconscious incompetence state," I added

I then added, "The fourth state is where we are going to get. Yes, your performance is automatic as you don't have to think about it and proceed to do it properly. You do it smoothly and rapidly. Maslow labeled this somewhat capable stage as 'unconscious competence.' And it usually occurs when the eyes are fine focused on a specific target."

Syd Thrift remarked, "So these pitchers' final stage of

learning a skill is when it becomes so natural they don't have to think about doing it?"

I could see the players were very interested in this learning concept, and I added," Once you are unconsciously competent you perform as if you are in the zone. You are free of thought and unaware of your body. It's the stage where you just focus on your target and let it happen."

I began, to summarize, my thoughts by slowing saying, "But you can't do it with your eyes closed or while wearing a blindfold. Your eyes are a big part of your performance, and they are a big part of your learning process."

I went on, "Even at the unconscious incompetence stage the motivation to do something is often because you see others doing it. And as your motivation pushes you into the conscious incompetence stage you begin to see that you are doing it right or reaching your goal. As you move to the conscious competence stage, you likely observe that even though you are conscious of doing it, you see you didn't succeed. You just weren't fast enough. But finally, as you move into the unconscious competent stage you use your eyes to focus on the appropriate target. As a result of pinpointed visual focus, your performance becomes an out-of-body experience."

I paused and then made a big emphasis, "The effect is that it will appear to you that the actions slow down, and the glove looks larger. You are highly visual, your body performs freely, naturally and rapidly. You have entered into the visual flow that takes you to the zone."

Buzzy Keller commented, "I like to fish in rivers near my home in Texas. Unconscious competence is the other shore, the bank on the opposite side of the vast river of conscious effort. All that practice has finally yielded dividends, and you can perform your skill without thinking; it comes naturally to you. It's the fourth and final stage that you call 'unconscious competence' but is what I call home."

I said, "Thanks, Buzzy, I don't know if it can't be stated

any better than that."

"These four steps or phases occurs whenever you attempt to achieve mastery. Any time you try to learn," I paused. "Now the level of your learning can be determined by how vivid your visual memory allows you to see yourself doing the action you are attempting to master."

I stopped and then made a greater emphasis by saying, "It helps to repeat your visual memory over and over again." Again, I was setting up for insights I would expand upon later.

Syd stood up and made a strong statement, "All of you pitchers in the Baseball Academy and you minor league pitchers you have a lot to learn. You have to learn how to improve your pitching mechanics. You have learned how to focus. You have to learn how to prepare. You have to learn how to adjust. You have to learn how to overcome adversity. You have to learn how to best pitch to the other hitters. If you are going to succeed as a pitcher, you are going to have to learn how to learn."

Syd paused and then said, "You guys have to learn how to learn. And if you apply what you have learned from Dr. Harrison you will be well on your way."

He looked around the room directly at the coaches and said, "And we have to learn how to teach these young pitchers so they can learn the game as fast as possible."

I added, "As competitors none of you like to fail. But you have to begin to see failure as an opportunity to learn. You can learn a lot from success, and you can learn a lot from failure. You can also learn a lot from others, how they handled their ups and their downs, even though they are totally different people and had a different set of circumstances."

Syd spoke up, "I agree. All of us coaches had a lot of failures. We learned, or we wouldn't be here instructing you, young guys. We want you to learn from our ups and downs."

He then looked at Academy pitching coach Chuck Stobbs and said, "Coach Stobbs you had a long career in the major leagues. You had great success, but you, unfortunately, pitched for a very poor team most of your career. Despite that do you think you could have benefitted at all from this understanding?"

Chuck took a few minutes to think about it and then said, "No doubt. If you pitchers can learn this while you are young, your career will be a lot more successful. If you are going to be successful, you have to learn how to learn. I did these things sometimes, but I didn't know what I was doing and why I was doing it. If I had have known what I was learning there is no doubt I would have had a much better won-loss record, even with the lousy team I was on."

After Chuck had finished his thoughts, I said, "So guys when you have pitched at your best, were you in a soft visual center or a fine visual center?" I asked.

"A fine visual center," Dennis Leonard spoke up and said quickly and then the others started nodding in agreement.

"When you are pitching in a fine visual center, how good are your results?" I paused. "In fact, when you were in a fine visual center how good were you physically, your mechanics?"

"Outstanding," said Dennis Leonard.

I followed with "When you were in a fine visual center how good was the mental side of your game?"

"I was at my best," said veteran minor league AAA pitcher, Jerry Cram.

I let that response resonate and then said, "So guys, what I want you to think about is that you when you learn to control your visual centering, adjusting it from the normal tendency of a soft visual center, to a fine visual center, you will improve the visual, the mental and the physical side of your game."

I went on, "So when you are doing your bullpens, you guys likely are trying to center on too many things at the same time. You simply cannot fully center on your leg action and your target at the same time. You need to select one task and center on that job solely."

Hal Baird asked, "What is more important visualizing the pitch or fine centering on the target?"

"That's a great question, Hal." I paused and added, "They are both importance because they help each other. You can throw pitchers by just fine centering, but if you want to be a pitcher you will gain by visualizing teach pitch in addition to fine centering on your target."

Changing direction, I made a bold statement "When you consider your pitching mechanics the most important consideration is what you are doing as the ball leaves your fingertips." I knew I had everyone confused and thinking about what I said.

I then demonstrated the position of being out over my front leg, "At that moment, you need to be fine centered on your specific target. By fine centering on your target at that moment, your body will have its best possible equilibrium."

I paused for a bit and then added, "As a result of best possible equilibrium you will have rhythm, capable of timing and will have relaxed fingers. In that manner, your pitch will have its best action."

"Because your body and subsequently your arm are relaxed, you will have less stress on your body and on your arm."

I paused and then said, "If you are in a soft center at the time of pitch release, your equilibrium will likely be compromised, and your body will get tighter. The resultant tightness in your shoulder and arm makes it very difficult to execute your mechanics correctly. Guys, I'm telling you that fine centering on your specific target is of great importance.

Chuck Stobbs spoke up, "That's the first time I ever heard of that and it is profound."

Syd Thrift said, "Amen to that. We need to focus on the desired endpoint, which this is, and then work backward. We've been going the wrong direction all the years."

He paused and then added, "That's true in pitching."

He looked at each of the coaches and then added, "But it is also relevant to hitting, bunting, fielding the ball, and throwing."

After a pause, Tom Bruno spoke up and asked. "I think I visualize the pitch when I need to make a good pitch. Why should I be concerned about visualizing every pitch?"

"Tom that is a great question. For many reasons, but it will help you get to that fine centered acute focus as you release the ball," I responded.

I then added, "You may be surprised that a high quality, accurate, realistic picture that encompasses feel and sight communicates the motor systems in your brain just what to do. It provides the brain and body a program to follow."

I let them digest the last statement and then added, "Furthermore by visualizing your pitch it keeps your focus on one thing. It doesn't allow you to think about other things."

Syd Thrift, "That's what I have been telling you guys for a long time. I think you guys are thinking about too many things."

He turned to Chuck Stobbs the Academy pitching coach, "Chuck, I want you to report to me daily in which one of the Academy pitchers on how they are centering on their task at hand."

Chuck nodded, and Syd added, "If their task at hand is mechanics in the bullpen let's not be concerned about the results of the pitch. The focus should be only whether they center correctly on the mechanical thing you want them to work on."

Syd was crafty. He wanted the Academy pitchers to know what his pitching coach's new assignment was to be. He knew the Academy pitchers loved Chuck Stobbs and would want to please him.

He then looked at the group of Academy pitchers and added, "Just like Dr. Harrison has said, you need to center your full attention on pitching a quality pitch through a specific target."

Syd paused and then exclaimed, "Now if you will apply what you hear from Dr. Harrison, you are going to have a chance to 'pitch lights out.'"

Concurring, I added, "You should be aware and make a decision on whether you want to center your attention in your body, on a mechanical aspect of your delivery or if you wish to center on your target. Ultimately you have that control and that responsibility."

I paused and looked in the direction of Coach Bill Fischer, "When your pitchers center within their body to refine a mechanical aspect of their delivery, they shouldn't at all be concerned about the quality or accuracy of their pitch." Fischer raised an eyebrow but didn't say anything.

I looked at the pitchers and said, "When you are working on mechanics your task at hand is about executing your mechanic properly. Your task at hand is not to throw a quality pitch to a specific target. In fact, if you choose to center your attention on your front side action, then don't be concerned about how the rest of your body performs or the quality of the pitch."

I then looked at Coach Fischer and said, "In this manner they will have a better focus on improving their mechanics." He smiled and seemed to be in agreement.

Steve Boros looked around the room and said, "Guys, from what Dr. Harrison has told, you now have a pathway on how to improve the visual side of the game, which will improve the mental side of your game. And I think you will probably find it is going to help the physical side of your game."

My final words were, "Guys that is it for today. We have really only covered what to consider doing. For those of you who are interested, we'll start working tomorrow on how to do it. There are some steps you can take to help you get into and maintain a fine center on your target."

I paused, "In simple terms, picture doing it, feel it, focus then pitch it through a specific target."

SlowTheGameDown's Player Performance Enhancement Program

SlowTheGameDown Visual Performance Training is based on the premise that "First and Foremost, Baseball is a Visual Game" and the belief that "Every pitch, play, and action should begin with what a player sees, and every play and every action should end with what a player visually focuses upon."

The training program consists of interdependent steps with a progression of emphasis for accomplishing the goal of seeing the ball better. Elements of the program include 1) Baseball-related visual skills assessment; 2) Training including on the field methods and concepts, in the hitting cage training methods and concepts; defensive play training methods and concepts, bullpen training methods, and concepts. 3) Baseball-related visual skills training; 4) Mobile equipment for the eyes and brain; and 5) Consultation, maintenance, and re-measurement,

Slow The Game Down's experience is in its fifth decade of development. Dr. Bill Harrison started with the Kansas City Royals in 1971, with George Brett, Hal McRae, Frank White, and in recent years with Barry Bonds, Greg Maddux, Jason Giambi, Mike Sweeney, Sean Casey, Edgar Renteria, Giancarlo Stanton and Hunter Pence. Ryan Harrison joined Bill in 1999 with the Cincinnati Reds and Atlanta Braves and has worked with many of the game's superstars including Carlos Beltran, Martin Prado, Angel Pagan, Hunter Pence, Michael Conforto, Carlos Delgado and Raul Ibanez.

The upside benefit of this training for a Major League team

is very significant. If players improve their defensive play or offensive production as Edgar Renteria and Andres Torres did in 2010; as Angel Pagan and Marco Scutaro did in 2012; and as Matt Duffy, Andrew Susac, Hunter Pence, and Gregor Blanco did in 2014; and as Ryan Goins, Kevin Pillar, Roberto Osuna, Aaron Sanchez, Chris Colabello, Matt Duffy, Jake Marisnick, Noah Syndegaard, Michael Conforto did in 2015; the added effort to enhance visual performance can be very valuable. Improvement of just a few players can have a major effect on an organization.

We have continued to expand our knowledge over the many years of working with players. We have been able to organize, simplify and communicate our approach to varying players' needs more effectively. We have developed practical tools that can be used, if desired, even within a game to achieve the player's visual focus needs. We've proven that players can increase the percentage of times have seen the ball early, identify it accurately, slow it down and track it deep to contact. This approach reduces visual errors that precede mental and physical errors and overall baseball performance improves.

A coordinated effort by the team owner, the front office, the manager, and coaches, along with the vision performance trainers provide a very significant on the team's "return on investment."

The Author's Baseball Background

"Who are you?" you should be asking. Whether you asked or not, I would like for you to know a bit about me. Very simply, I've had a passion for this game since I was three. I loved throwing and hitting a ball, any ball, large or small.

My early years in school were focused on being an athlete and getting good enough grades to get into college. With a combination baseball-academic scholarship to the University of California at Berkeley, I accomplished my early life's goal. But my real goal was to be a major league baseball player.

Well, I didn't make it. However, in 1971 I pioneered some unique ideas into Major League Baseball. It led to a career of over 40 years working with top players in the game.

And I got decent enough at it to receive a full ride scholarship to the University of California at Berkeley. I played until I was 21. An injury derailed my upward bound career.

Some of my most memorable fun days as a child were listening to games on the radio and acting them out. I listened to so many Cleveland Indians games that it seemed as the players had become my friends. I experienced success and failure with each one of their efforts in the games I listened to Al Rosen, Roberto Avila, Luke Easter, Gene Woodling, Lou Boudreaux, George Strickland, Bob Feller, Bob Lemon, Mike Garcia, Herb Score, Mel Harder, Jim Hegan, Dale Mitchell, Larry Doby, Satchel Paige, Joe Gordon, Ray Boone, and Ken Keltner were my virtual friends in the theater of my mind! I remember enacting out the hitting a lot of home runs as a Cleveland Indian in Yankee Stadium.

From the age nine to twelve I had considerable success playing the game of my era, baseball rules with a lightweight, 10-inch rubber coated ball. We never scuffed the leather of a baseball, but we softened the rubber cover of the ball. I loved pitching the 10 inch because of it being lightweight the ball would dive in, out and down as if I was Yu Darvish. My town, you may laugh at this, had 800 to 1000 residents when the migrant workers arrived to pick the cotton. Our K-8 school had a total of about 125 students. We played other elementary schools, and we usually won. All we did was play baseball. There wasn't much else to do in the barren San Joaquin Valley farm towns.

My most fun was playing pickup games in a powdery dust field in the hot 100-110 degree days. At night, indoors we often hit ping pong balls with a rolled up magazine and had a terrific time. I further refined my eye-hand coordination hitting gravel pellets with a stick into an open field. I tossed my share of hard dirt clods at targets also. I know that when I played the game as a kid, I could hit anything and everything, and I could throw accurately.

In fact, when I was in the seventh grade I remember a game in McFarland, California. Our Alpaugh Elementary seventh grade team crushed them. I remember hitting three home runs. The third occurred after the coach instructed the pitcher to bounce the ball near home plate. I saw the ball bounce and proceeded to hit another long home run. The game sure seemed easy back then.

I could play this game a little bit. I was a Little League and Babe Ruth League phenom. Because I matured physically rapidly, I was 5'll" and 185 lbs. In the eighth grade, my physical attributes made this game rather easy for me. I was the number one starting pitcher and when not pitching the starting first baseman for four varsity seasons.

I was a starting varsity player for four years at Bullard High School in Fresno and received All-League and All-City honors three of those years. I received four varsity baseball letters and a total of eleven varsity letters in three sports.

I had a phenomenal coach during my junior and senior year in High school. Coach Bob Bennett. Coach Bennett later won 1302 games as head coach at Fresno State University and was inducted into the Association of College Baseball Coaches Hall of Fame. I was really lucky to have Coach Bennett help me develop my baseball skills.

Later I was a starting pitcher and had the team leading batting average on a California State Championship Junior College team. At Fresno City College, I was a member of two teams that became state champions. Because California had the best junior college baseball teams during that time, we arguably were the number one team in the nation, though there was not such a ranking system at that time. At Fresno City College, I learned to love winning.

The following two years I pitched and eventually became the number one pitcher at the University of California at Berkeley, with a low ERA. My two-year ERA was 2.07, the 7th lowest in Cal Bear history, but my won-loss record was only 6-4. We didn't score many runs. At Cal, I learned to hate losing.

I enjoyed a shutout victory over Stanford in 1964, the first shutout in the Cal-Stanford series that had started forty years earlier. A shutout was not pitched in that series for another thirty years. So I pitched the only shutout in 70 years of the series.

My biggest disappointment with college baseball was, as a pitcher, not being able to take batting practice to prepare for games. I quickly became a .150 Hitter and the ball looked like a pea. At Cal, I had to focus fully on being a pitcher because I had a lively arm and could throw strikes.

Along the way, I played with future major leaguers Wade Blasingame, Andy Messersmith, Dick Selma, Mike Epstein, Rich Nye, Dave Dowling and Larry Colton. In youth leagues, high school, and college I played against Tom Seaver, Jim

Fregosi, Bob Garibaldi, Jim Lonborg, Pat Corrales, Darrell and Gary Sutherland, Randy Schwartz, Nelson Briles, John Boccabella and others.

I was proud. I was headed to the show. However, a shoulder injury derailed my dreams. Surgeons weren't saving baseball players careers back in that day.

So I went on a search. I decided to become a Doctor of Optometry. And with that decision I had as a secondary goal that I was going to find out what made the difference between the famed Ted Williams, the last of the .400 Hitters and other players. Was it his outstanding eyesight, his extraordinary depth perception, or his phenomenal accurate and speed of recognition? I was going to find out as I studied optometry.

There were some key moments in my baseball career that shaped my understanding that I am going to share with you in this book. I probably learned as much or more from my failures than I did from my successes. My main talent was that I could paint the low outside corner with my slider and for whatever reason my fastball was difficult to hit hard. I did throw some no-hitters in high school and had a five for five day in a junior college game, so I know a little bit about success. Simply, I performed without conscious thought. On the other hand, I had some days I've tried to forget. I never could accept failing or losing.

Little did I know that my career in professional baseball would not be as a player but would be as a consultant, a vision coach and that I would have the opportunity to work with many of the game's All-Stars as well as future Hall of Fame inductees. I've been working with MLB players over forty years and am now ready to share my insights on what works and what didn't work.

Since I became infatuated with the game, it has certainly changed. When I started working with major league players they each were making around $15-20,000 and were hungry for information that could help them. Today MLB clubhouses are full of multi-millionaires. But in many respects, the players haven't changed.

How2Focus: **The Pitchers Zone**

Dr Bill Harrison

His work in professional baseball began in 1971 with the Kansas City Royals. Baseball Hall of Fame star George Brett was among the first players he trained. Since that time he has worked with 15 MLB organizations, and many NCAA baseball programs. Most recently he and his company have worked with the Toronto Blue Jays and 2014, 2012, 2010 World Champions San Francisco Giants. Among the coaches and baseball leaders who participated in his training programs were Jack McKeon, Syd Thrift, Rex Bowen, Branch Rickey, Jr, John Schuerholz, Charley Lau, Mel Didier, Harry Dunlap, Karl Kuehl and Bam-Bam Meulens. College coaches include Augie Garrido, Gene Stephenson, Bob Bennett, John Scolinos, Andy Lopez, Pat Casey and many others. Through the years he has worked hundreds of baseball stars including position players, Lou Piniella, Frank White, Rod Carew and Tony Gwynn in the 1980's, Sammy Sosa, Barry Bonds, Jason Giambi, and Shawn Green in the '90's; Carlos Beltran, Mike Sweeney, Sean Casey, Jose Guillen, Jonny Gomes, Raul Ibanez, Jayson Werth, Adam Dunn, Angel Pagan, Giancarlo Stanton, Rajai Davis and Hunter Pence in the 2000's. Pitchers include Paul Splittorff, Ron Bryant, and Bert Blyleven in the 1970's, Doug Drabek, Steve Trachsel, and Pete Harnisch in the 90's; Greg Maddux, Jason Johnson, Mark Hendrickson, Bronson Arroyo and Danny Graves in the 2000's; Daniel Norris, Aaron Sanchez, Justin Nicolino, Matt Boyd, Noah Syndergaard, and Drew Hutchinson in the 2010's. Many consider him to be one of this country's premier minds for sports enhancement as countless world-class athletes prepare for competition with Dr. Harrison's concepts in their training programs.

Ryan Harrison

Ryan has a degree in Exercise Physiology from University of California at Davis. Ryan has worked with Dr. Bill Harrison on improving athlete's visual performance on the field. He currently working with the Toronto Blue Jays and the 2014, 2012, and 2010 World Champions San Francisco Giants. He previously has worked with Philadelphia Phillies 2009-2012 as well as 9 other Professional Baseball Organizations over the last 14 years. Collegiately he has worked with the 2013 NCAA Champions UCLA Bruins, as well as Oregon State, Dallas Baptist, Wichita State, Kentucky, Long Beach State, and U of Arizona Baseball Programs. Ryan has worked with many Collegiate Softball programs, individual athletes in various sports such as MMA, Motocross, NHL, NFL, WTA, AVP, PGA. Following his work with top professional and amateur athletes, he conceived the idea of training necessary performance skills with digital technology. The STGD Athlete APP and SportsEyesite™ Software are a result of his goal to develop training products so that everyone could benefit at a fraction of the cost of having this training and without the need to go to a specialty clinic. He has personally trained over 100 major league roster players on the visual side of the game—among the major League players he has trained includes Shawn Green, Carlos Delgado, Carlos Beltran, Mike Sweeney, Raul Ibanez, Jayson Werth, Angel Pagan, Hunter Pence, Delmon Young, John Baker, Jerry Hairston, Jr., Kevin Pillar, Ryan Goins, Matt Duffy, Andrew Susac, Josh Willingham, Jonny Gomes, Rajai Davis, Colby Rasmus, Jose Reyes and others.